Asking
For
Trouble

Asking For Trouble

Understanding
what people *think* when
you can't trust what they *say*

Jon Cohen

WONDER WHEEL
PUBLISHING

Wonder Wheel Publishing
Lower Ground Floor
105 Piccadilly
London
W1J 7NJ

First printed in Great Britain in 2021

Cover Design by Jack Smyth
Interior design by Adam Hay Studio

Printed and bound in Great Britain
by Clays Ltd, Elcograf S.p.A

A CIP catalogue record for this book is
available from the British Library

ISBN: 978-1-8381199-1-1

www.wonderwheelpublishing.com

To my sons
It can be done

CONTENTS

Introduction

It all started with a picture of a dead cat. My first task as a market researcher was to ask people what they thought about a black and white image of a scrawny cat with a bolt through its head. The question was simple: Did the image cross the line? Would the advertising shock people into connecting with the cause, or was it a picture of cruelty so disturbing as to turn the public off?

Some twenty-five years on, I've asked over ten thousand people what they think about almost every challenge we face as a society and every product we consume. From teenage pregnancy to tissues and from cars to cancer, you name it, I've researched it. Through it all, one constant theme has dominated my working life:

> Asking is easy. The hard part is knowing
> what to do with the answer.

These are the questions I've been grappling with since my lunch with a dead cat. When you ask people for their thoughts and feelings:

- How do you choose who to listen to and who to ignore?

- How do you resolve conflicting and contradictory responses?

- How do you even know if the people you are asking are telling you the truth?

- How do you use the answers to make good decisions rather than bad?

It's only natural to ask people what they think. It is not possible to create, build, launch or do something of value without asking your intended audience for their opinion. And yet, in both our personal and professional lives, we regularly receive confusing feedback, mixed messages and unreliable responses, and then we're confronted with the challenge of working out what to do next.

The ability to interpret response has never been more important than it is today. As we begin to develop ideas in a post-Covid world, we cannot presume to know what people want, feel and think. The most successful businesses are invariably those best able to satisfy the changing needs of their customers. The finest marketing campaigns perfectly capture the prevailing mood of their target audience. Now is the time to invest in insight, empathy and understanding. Fortunately, we are blessed with instant access to more feedback than we have ever had before. Social media platforms have dramatically increased the opportunities for the public to share their opinions. The inseparable relationship people have with their mobile phones makes it possible for them to record their instinctive in-the-moment reactions to ideas as they go about their daily lives. The pandemic has accelerated the adoption of video calling as the new home for conversation, making it significantly more convenient for businesses to connect with their consumers across the globe. And yet, despite the wealth of feedback at our fingertips, it doesn't get any easier to work out what to do with the response. In an increasingly opinion-rich digital world, it becomes ever harder to understand what people truly think of our ideas and make good decisions as a result.

Let *Asking for Trouble* be your guide as you travel through a land that is both enlightening and disorientating, in equal measure. It is a tale of three parts:

1. Understanding

2. Truth

3. A Guide to Good Asking

Part One introduces an analytical framework designed to help you better interpret response. Part Two describes an approach to asking that will get you closer to the truth.

And Part Three provides practical advice, hints and tips on how to get the most out of the experience of asking.

There is another part to the story. And that part is you. You are the golden thread that runs through every page of this book. My aim is not only to demonstrate the vital role you play in understanding response and getting closer to the truth, but also, to encourage you to better balance your own instincts with other people's opinions, and ultimately, empower you to have more confidence in yourself and the decisions you make.

Whether you're a marketing director striving to grow your brands, an entrepreneur nurturing a new concept, a policymaker hoping to build a brighter world, an eager market researcher foisting images of emaciated animals on an unsuspecting public, or you've got a good idea and you want to know what people think; this book is for you.

Part One

UNDERSTANDING

'Words are illusions'

Bodhidharma: Founder of Zen Buddhism

1

The Illusion of Interest

S ome years ago, I spent the summer talking to troubled teenagers about sex. I needed to get their opinions on a range of ideas designed to encourage young men and women to consider contraception, and to think carefully about the consequences of unprotected sex.

Everything was set fair. I was perched on a leather footstool in the living room of a small two-up two-down, in a forgotten housing estate at the heart of a broken seaside town. It was a warm summer's afternoon, and the open patio doors welcomed a gentle sea breeze into the modest room that served as my place of work for the day.

My first four boys turned up, a tight-knit group of friends who lived in care. There's an inextricable link between poverty and teenage pregnancy, and these lads were from tough backgrounds. Welcoming the boys into the living room, I sat them down on the sofas, handed over their financial incentive and introduced myself. The boys looked at each other, they looked at me, then back at each other – and they were gone. Through the open patio doors, clambering over the six-foot garden wall and away with the cash. Never to be seen again.

Lesson one: Asking people what they think of an idea relies heavily on having people to ask.

My next session was more successful. I met Finn.

Finn was seventeen, and he was a dad. Kaylie, his daughter, was two, but he didn't have much to do with her. Finn still saw his own father, lying by the bins as you turned left out of the lifts, a life destroyed by hard memories and harder drugs. Chatting together on that warm summer's afternoon, it wasn't hard to ask Finn what he thought. He was one of the smartest young men I had ever met and he had plenty to say. Asking was easy.

So, here's the question.

Which of the two experiences of asking better reflects how people engage with ideas in the real world? The desperate leap over the garden wall or the conscientious living-room conversation? It's no contest. Leaping lads beat friendly Finn every time. That is the trouble with asking. The interest shown in our ideas is an illusion.

Ask people what they think, and they focus. It makes no difference whether you're talking to a friend over a cup of coffee, seeking advice from a highly qualified team of experts, thoughtfully exploring the pros and cons of your idea in depth interviews, discussing alternative creative concepts with potential customers in research groups, or questioning one thousand anonymous souls online; the act of asking encourages people to pay attention to your idea in a way that is totally out of sync with how they would behave in the real world.

Whatever the nature of your idea, be it an app or an advert, a product or policy, business or book, successful asking starts with the acceptance of this simple principle:

When we ask people what they think, the focus on our idea creates an illusion of interest. They have only engaged because we have asked them to.

The illusion of interest is an inevitable and unavoidable consequence of asking people what they think. To make good decisions based on other people's opinions, we must first acknowledge that the world of asking is a land of make-believe. Think of it like this. When we ask people for feedback, we're having a nice, intelligent chat with Finn. But the conversation is an illusion. In the real world, our intended audience has jumped over the garden wall and is legging it down the street. And that makes all the difference.

The Disappearing Robot

Leaning on a cardboard cut-out of a digital robot with an oversized head, Abdi smokes a quick cigarette before our chat. He searches for an ashtray, but all he can find is a plastic cup resting precariously on a small pouch – packed with information leaflets – that protrudes from the cardboard robot's tiny waist. It'll do. Abdi drops his cigarette into the pool of coffee lying at the bottom of the cup and ambles over to join the group.

You might recognise the happy robot stood by the double doors, welcoming all comers to the Selby Centre: a multicultural community hub in the bustling heart of Tottenham, North London.

His name is DigitAl (Digit Al, get it?), and he was the centrepiece of an enormous multimedia campaign that accompanied the UK's switch to digital TV, finally completed in October 2012. For years, Al was everywhere: on TV, social media, posters, newspapers, bus sides and bus stops. You couldn't miss him.

Al did a good job of communicating the information the public required for a smooth switchover, with one exception. For some reason, critical messages didn't seem to be getting through to poorer, immigrant communities around the UK. Something wasn't working. Digital UK, the government body set up to manage the switchover, held countless research groups to try and understand why. Abdi and his friends gathered around large, life-size cardboard cut-outs of Al before the start of the group, sharing with him their stories, cigarettes and empty coffee cups.

Yet moments later, when asked what they thought of the advertising featuring DigitAl, they didn't recognise him. More than that, they were certain they had never seen him before. DigitAl was invisible. He did not exist.

But even more surprising was the reaction of Abdi and his friends when asked, 'What do you think of Al?' They loved him. They couldn't get enough of him. Al went from invisible robot to best friends forever in the blink of a sixty-second ad. It was like flicking a switch. Their real relationship with DigitAl and their requested response were polar opposites. The four little words, 'What do you think?' changed everything.

If you hadn't witnessed the group participants physically leaning on DigitAl only moments earlier, you would have been convinced their love for Al was real. You would have been one hundred per cent certain the poor awareness of switchover communications amongst particular ethnic communities in the UK was the result of insufficient and ineffective media spend – the right people simply hadn't seen enough of Al. But you would have been wrong. For them, DigitAl was an irrelevance, a cartoon coffee cup holder at best. All the media money in the world wouldn't have made the slightest difference.

Ask Abdi and his pals what they think of Al, and their answer is, 'He's lovely. I'd like to take him home to meet my wife.' But the real answer should be, 'What is this nonsense? What's it got to do with me? Where's the ashtray?'

Double Trouble...

Year in year out, the switch to digital technology continues to redefine the way we live, work, play and of course, ask. Yet, no matter how much the process of gathering opinions or the context for the conversation may change, at the very core of asking there remains one constant unerring truth: We cannot trust the response. Whether we're chatting via video from the safety of our own homes or sitting together in the same cosy living room by the seaside, when we ask people what they think of an idea, they focus. And the focus

8

changes their response. The stark reality is that the revised response may not just be a minor distortion of their true feelings, it may be completely wrong, diametrically opposed to the way they would feel about our ideas in the real world.

Success or Failure

There are many reasons why businesses and marketing concepts fail to live up to expectation. Chief among them is an inability to meet their customers' needs. When push comes to shove, the intended audience are not interested in what they are being shown, told or sold. Yet, in every instance, the idea owner will ask, 'What do you think?' They'll run focus groups, commission surveys and discuss their ideas with a wealth of colleagues, friends and family. They'll ask and ask and ask. And yet, the majority will still launch an idea, product or service destined to disappoint. How is that possible? Something must be going wrong with the asking. Something fundamental.

The trouble is those doing the asking believe the response to be real. They take the feedback at face value. They fall for the illusion that people are interested in their ideas and they don't understand how the asking distorts the answer. The illusion of interest may be an inevitable and unavoidable consequence of asking people what they think, but it's a misdirection, an artifice, a con, a trick. Like all magic, it's not real. One puff, and it's gone.

Bad Habits

I wanted to know what Abdi thought of an idea designed to promote NHS Stop Smoking Services. I found him in the car park, trying to stuff a six-foot cardboard robot into the boot of his car. This is what I showed him:

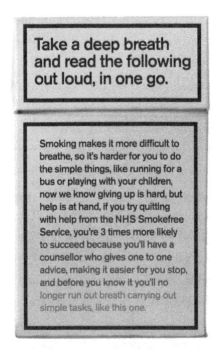

Smoker or not, have a go. See if you can get to the end without taking a breath.

What do you think of the idea? It's clever, isn't it? Getting smokers involved in a breathing task is a smart way of encouraging them to engage in a message they might otherwise reject.

Since I have your attention:

- Do you think the copy could do with being a bit shorter?

- Would the idea work best as an on-pack warning or a Facebook ad?

- Is the message of support sufficiently clear?

- How good a job does it do of promoting NHS Stop Smoking Services?

All perfectly sensible questions which would doubtless prompt insightful and instructive answers. Shame the entire exercise is a waste of breath. Like you, a smoker would only connect with the concept because they have been asked to read it. In the real world, smokers are unlikely to even register the idea, let alone participate in the task they have been asked to complete.

Yet that is exactly what we do when we ask people what they think. We show them our ideas, pose intelligent questions and listen attentively to the answer, conveniently overlooking the fact that everything we have learnt is founded on a fantasy.

The illusion of interest is so hard to resist. When we ask for feedback, our starting point is that our ideas are worthy of interest. The oversized response makes sense to us because of the largeness of the idea in our own minds. Even if we recognise the interest in our idea to be an illusion, it is almost impossible to resist the temptation to believe it to be real. Like smoking, just because we know something is bad for us doesn't mean we don't do it. We do. We breathe in the interest deeply, exhale, and come back for more.

It's time to quit!

And what better time to start than now?

It's as natural to ask people what they think as it is to breathe. But we can no longer afford to let the answers suffocate our ideas and stunt their growth. Thankfully, *Asking for Trouble* is on hand to help. It will give you all the support you need to properly get to grips with the illusion of interest. Part One will enable you to better interpret response, Part Two will bring you closer to the truth and Part Three will guide you on your way.

An unpredictable and ever-evolving world requires timeless solutions to fundamental problems. My purpose is to provide you with an enduring set of principles and practical tools for asking, designed to enhance understanding, improve decision-making and facilitate the development of desirable ideas. The lessons to be learnt are intended to remain as relevant for tomorrow as they are for today. However troublesome tomorrow may be.

Jump On

I have a special sense of affinity with the young boys that jumped the garden wall, because as well as being a market researcher, I also happen to be the father of four boys. When my kids were little, every night as I kissed them goodnight, they asked, 'Where did you go today, Daddy?'

'I went to a wonderful world of fantasy and make-believe,' I replied.

'How did you get there?' they asked, amazed.

'I flew there,' I told them mysteriously. 'On the magic carpet Mummy and I brought back from the ancient city of Marrakesh.'

And it was true. Sort of. The world of asking has been my second home for nearly twenty-five years. It is indeed a strange and wonderful land filled with enchantment and mystery. Come with me on my journey of discovery. There's plenty of room on my carpet for two.

2

Response and Responsibility

'The price of greatness is responsibility'

Winston Churchill

There is an illusion as old as time itself. It is called the moon illusion, and it describes how the moon appears to be larger when it is near the horizon than when it is higher in the sky. Of course, the moon is not actually larger; it just looks it.

Theories and explanations abound, yet the moon illusion remains unresolved. From Aristotle to Descartes, the brightest stargazers, the finest scientists and the most brilliant of minds have tried to figure it out, but none have been able to explain how the illusion works.

Here's the thing – and you might remember this from when you were a child – if you turn your back to the moon, bend over and look between your legs, the moon illusion almost entirely disappears. I kid you not. It just goes to show, if you view the world from a different perspective, oversized illusions and seemingly insurmountable problems can simply disappear.

A New Perspective

The world of asking currently works like this:

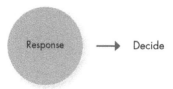

We ask people what they think and decide what to do based on the feedback we receive. Whether our decision is to press on, abandon ship, refine or revise, the changes we make are driven by the response. In our world of asking, where we embrace the principle that the interest shown in our idea is an illusion, that straight-line system of decision-making doesn't work. It is impossible to go directly from A to B, because there is no line between the two.

This simple fact demands a fundamental shift in the way in which we ask for, listen to, think about and act upon other people's opinions. Rather than trying to leap mindlessly from response to decision, there is an extra step we need to take – the responsibility step.

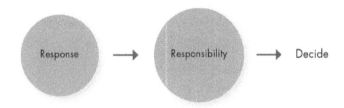

When we ask people what they think, we should listen to the answer and then ask ourselves, 'What does the response mean?' That is our responsibility. The quality of the decisions we make based on the opinions of others will, therefore, be entirely dependent on the extent to which we take our responsibilities seriously.

In his book, *The 7 Habits of Highly Effective People*, Stephen Covey suggested that to achieve different outcomes, we should see the world from a different paradigm and behave accordingly. Well, in the world of asking, this is our paradigm shift:

> **What people think of our ideas is
> not what matters most. It is what we
> do with the answer that counts.**

To get the most out of the experience of asking, we need to put our responsibilities above the response itself.

Driving Responsibly

By making development decisions based directly on other people's feedback, we lose control of our idea. It's as if we have handed the car keys to our prospective customers and given them licence to decide both the direction of travel and our eventual destination.

If you're lucky, it will work out fine.

Chances are, it won't.

Given that eighty per cent of businesses fail within the first three years, should you choose to take the traditional approach to asking, it is safe to assume that most of the time, you'll find yourself a passenger in a car on the road to nowhere.[1] But then, if you let someone else drive your idea, you can hardly be surprised if they lead you down a path you don't want to go.

Assuming responsibility for understanding response is liberating because we take back the power to decide the direction of our ideas. The gathering together of opinions is merely the first step on our journey. The second requires us to build a bridge between the asked-for answers and the real-world. It's a much tougher task, but the rewards are great. Instead of being swayed and buffeted by the opinions of others, we can begin to use the asking to help us make decisions that will maximise the potential of our ideas in the real, rather than imagined, world. It's not that we don't care what other people think. We do. We care enormously. We're just not letting them drive the car.

This is the moment of your emancipation. To get the most out of asking, all you have to do is make the effort to understand the answer. The aim is to get to a point where your ability to interpret response is as natural as the asking itself. Of course, there is an alternative. You could always turn around, bend over and ask with your head between your legs. I've tried it a few times, and to be honest, the results were mixed.

'Wonder is the beginning of wisdom'

Socrates

3

The Wonder Wheel

The Wonder Wheel is a framework designed to help you better interpret response. It is made up of the seven wonders of the world of asking and has a heart of desire. Everything you could want and need to know about your idea is contained within the wheel.

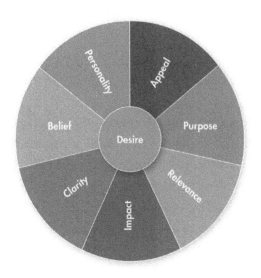

The principle underpinning the framework is simple. When we ask people what they think of our ideas, we rarely have just the one big question in mind. Typically, we want to know the following:

- Appeal: Do you like my idea? What do you like about it? What don't you like?

- Purpose: What is the point of my idea? What does it do? What needs does it fulfil?

- Relevance: Can you relate to the idea? How does it fit into your life? What does it mean to you?

- Impact: Does my idea stand out? Is it distinctive?

- Clarity: Do you understand the idea?

- Belief: Is it credible? Will it do the job?

- Personality: How does my idea come across? What are its values? How would you describe it?

- Desire: Do you want my idea? Do you find it motivating? Would you buy it?

Desire sits at the heart of the wheel for two reasons. Firstly, the central aim of asking is to make an idea more enticing, to create an object of desire. Secondly, the desirability of an idea is a function of its appeal, purpose, relevance, impact, clarity, believability and personality combined. The more effort we make to understand the response in all its glory, the more compelling our ideas will therefore be.

Working the Wheel

Depending on the nature of your idea, the specific questions will change, yet the essential elements of the wheel remain the same. Let me give you an example:

What do you think of this headline for a new travel guide app?[2]

Stuff Your Eyes With Wonder
See The World
Download The App

The simple question, 'What do you think?' is shorthand for: Do you like the headline? What is the message? Can you relate to the sentiment? Does it stand out? Is the communication clear? Is it believable? How does the brand come across? All in all, do you want to find out more?

However, if we were to ask people for their thoughts on the app itself, the questions would be different: Do you like the way it looks? When would you use it? Does it meet your needs? How does it compare to other travel apps? Is it simple to use? Do you have confidence the app will do the job? All in all, would you download it?

As you can see, the questions and the responses will differ depending on the subject, yet the structure of the wheel remains the same. For our travel app, clarity refers to navigation or comprehension, depending on whether we are asking about product design or communication.

All you need do is adapt the questions to suit your specific requirements. Turning the wheel should be easy and intuitive because the wonders are natural. They simply represent the questions you would instinctively ask and reflect the answers you would expect to hear. For further examples, head to askingfortrouble.net, where you'll find dedicated questions for a wide range of ideas and scenarios.

Learning to Steer

Adopting the Wonder Wheel as an analytical framework to help you navigate your way through the world of asking has a number of advantages.

Firstly, the Wonder Wheel is a checklist. When you ask people what they think, it's tempting to get stuck on one part of the response – for instance, how much they like the idea – and overlook some of the other important attributes that could contribute to your future success. At its most basic, the framework gives you confidence and certainty. You can be sure the essential questions will be covered and the gaps in your knowledge will be filled.

Secondly, the wonders of the wheel add depth and colour to the generic, superficial phrases that so often characterise response. For example:

'Nice idea'

'Seems good'

'It looks cheap'

When it comes to developing ideas, bland opinions do not help. You need to know what it is about your idea, concept or product that makes it look cheap, seem good or appear interesting. Similarly, lifeless language such as 'good quality' or 'value for money' is almost entirely useless when working out how to enhance the desirability of an idea. By breaking the response down, you can engage in a more meaningful assessment of the ways in which people do, or do not, connect with your idea. The wheel gives you the impetus to explore further and gain a deeper, richer understanding of what people really think.

Thirdly, the Wonder Wheel will help you determine priorities. For example, although the purpose of your idea may be obvious, people could be uncertain about its relevance for them. Your communication may be crystal clear, but the tone of voice may be inappropriate for your brand. Using a framework to interpret response enables you to hone in on what matters most, focus on areas of weakness and highlight opportunities for development.

Here Comes Trouble

While the Wonder Wheel encourages us to ask the right questions, brings response to life and draws our attention to critical issues, we would still be crazy to follow the route suggested by our super new consumer-friendly sat nav. Why? Because the response isn't real.

Splitting the illusion of interest into seven segments doesn't make it any less of an illusion. In fact, the reverse is true. The Wonder Wheel reveals what we are up against and alerts us to the troubles that lie in store.

Imagine walking into a fairground house of mirrors, the reflection in each of the mirrors giving you a different sense of yourself. It's fun, but false. Similarly, when we ask people what they think, every wonder is altered by the act of asking in its own unique way. However, unlike the ridiculous images entertaining us at the fairground, the distortions we will inevitably encounter on our quest of discovery tend to be more subtle. And even if we see the responses for what they are – an absurd exaggeration of the truth – we are often so taken with the image staring back at us that we overlook the fact we don't have legs up to our elbows or a waist the size of a Marvel superhero.

To make matters more difficult, at the heart of the wheel sits the grand illusion of desire – the coming together of seven misconceptions, false impressions and delusions. It's little wonder, therefore, that asking so often ends in disarray. The nugget of knowledge we yearn for the most is the likeliest to lead us astray.

Finding the Way

The purpose of the Wonder Wheel goes way beyond defining the questions we need to ask and determining the answers we should seek. That's the easy part. The challenge is to understand what people think of our ideas in a world where we can't trust what they say. That is the beauty of the framework. It is designed to expose the deceptions in all their glory and help us get to grips with the distortions that define response.

Assuming you believe your customers should have a voice in the development of your ideas, you have a choice. You can either pretend everything they have to say is real, or you can embrace and resolve the illusions that will accompany you on your journey through the world of asking. Whether the opinions of others drive you down a dark alley or towards a brighter future is entirely in your hands. After all, you're the one holding the wheel.

4

Appeal

What do you think of my idea?
Do you like it?
What do you like about it?
What don't you like?

S ociety is obsessed with appeal. Likes, loves, thumbs
up, thumbs down, smiley faces, sad faces – all the
time, everywhere. Often, 'What do you think?' is a
thinly disguised synonym for 'Do you like?'

We are dazzled and bewitched by appeal, and that is
asking for trouble. It's not that appeal doesn't matter. It
does. In the real world, we connect most with the things
we like. The problem is the illusion that being liked in the
world of asking is the same as being wanted in the real
world. It is not.

The Greatest Show on Earth

It's the spring of 2012 and London is buzzing. In only a few short months the Olympics are coming to town. Oh, and the Paralympics, of course.

For the first time ever, the Paralympics Organising Committee awarded the UK exclusive broadcast rights of the London 2012 Paralympic Games to Channel 4, rather than the BBC. The thinking behind the decision was that, as broadcaster of the Olympics proper, the BBC could not help but view the Paralympics as second best. It was a masterstroke. For Channel 4, the Paralympics stood alone. For them, it was the big one – the most significant sporting event in the history of Channel 4 television. They were proud to be the broadcaster and committed to its success. For the launch campaign, the team at Channel 4 came up with the following three ideas:

Idea One: The human side of disability
Idea One confronted the hidden subjects of disability: taboo topics such as 'Can a paraplegic have sex?' The ads featured Paralympians telling personal stories in a way that was both searingly honest and utterly compelling.

Idea Two: Gladiators
The second idea was based on the film, *Gladiator*. It was an unabashed, full-throttle big event advertising concept: sport as competitive and unmissable gladiatorial combat.

Idea Three: Superhumans

This idea revolved around a sci-fi vision of Paralympians as athletes on another level. The Iron Man-esque fusion of technology and human creating something superhuman.

The response in research was unequivocal. People loved the Gladiator idea. It was a celebration of the Paralympics in a way the British public had not experienced before: an intoxicating mix of what they wanted to see in a great sporting event, applied to the world of disability.

Conversely, the concept of bringing the human side of disability into people's living rooms proved predictably unsettling. Yet there seemed to be little to be gained from the discomfort caused. Sports fans found it hard to engage with the emotional stories and the audiences less inclined to watch sport failed to get excited about the big event. The idea fell between two stools.

And then there was the Superhumans. People hated it. The response was resolutely negative. Across the entire sample, a single lone voice offered a different perspective. One young man initially rejected the idea, then stopped himself, and said:

> *"To be honest, I think the real reason I don't like it is because it doesn't fit with how I feel about Paralympians. I don't think they're as great as able-bodied athletes and that's not right. I still don't like the sci-fi thing, but this idea makes the Paralympics sound amazing. I can't wait."*

Deep down, Superhumans did not reflect how people felt about Paralympians. They viewed them in a lesser light than able-bodied Olympians. In truth, until 2012, the dominant emotion was one of pity. Superhumans said something different. Paralympians were supreme athletes that had gone beyond the normal limits of effort, endurance, commitment and sporting excellence. They exceeded the boundaries of us mere mortals; they *were* superhuman.

Superhumans was a 'more than human' concept in a 'less than human' world.

The advertising campaign embodied everything that Channel 4 was trying to achieve. Superhumans did not just put the Paralympics on a par with the Olympics, it took it to a whole new level. Respondents had a fundamental issue with the very essence of the Superhuman concept because it didn't fit with their current view of the world – a view that had to change. The reason why the Superhuman idea was rejected was the very reason why the ad had to be made.

But that is not all. The high-tech, Iron man-esque, depiction of Paralympians and their equipment was also partly responsible for people's lack of engagement with the idea. In this instance, their reservations needed to be heard. The depersonalised glorification of wheelchairs and blades required rethinking. The athlete needed to be more important than the kit.

Some of the dislike was helpful, some of it was not. When you ask people what they think of your idea, thumbs up, thumbs down, smiley face, sad face, doesn't do the job. Appeal is not a straightforward concept.

The final Superhuman ad was much loved. And it worked! Eighty-seven per cent of people who saw the campaign went on to watch the Paralympics. Fifty-six per cent of viewers felt more comfortable talking about disabilities. And eighty-five per cent of those who saw the advertising thought of disabled athletes as being as talented as non-disabled athletes. The launch campaign for the Paralympics was named 'Campaign of the Year', and it remains the most remarkable and humbling project I have worked on.

Rather than being seen as 'the bit after the Olympics' involving people that elicit pity, the Paralympics became an event contested by athletes who inspired awe and admiration. In the space of just a few weeks, Channel 4's *Meet the Superhumans* campaign changed how people in this country viewed disability sport – perhaps forever. Based on its appeal in research, the advertising would never have been made.

The Consequences of Liking Appeal Too Much

There's nothing wrong with wanting people to like your ideas, but if you put love on a pedestal you're asking for trouble. Many ideas fail because the appeal during their development was strong and the positive response was mistakenly assumed to be a good indicator of success. Liking stuff matters, but it's a start at best. The decisions we make based on how much people like our ideas are often wrong. People like the familiar and the similar. We prefer things not to change and avoid risk. When asked, 'What do you think?' we subconsciously choose to like the ideas that enable us to stay right where we are. To do nothing. To think nothing new. The Gladiator ad was embraced with enthusiasm because it represented a glorified version of the status quo.

When asked what we think about new concepts, we are programmed to promote the development of those ideas that are going to be easiest for us to ignore in the real world. This has a couple of important implications:

1. The more your idea challenges the way people behave, the more unreliable 'liking' becomes. Given that we want our ideas to work, it doesn't therefore, make much sense to be so hung up on such a poor indicator of success.

2. The spikey, jagged edges that differentiate your idea will almost certainly be rejected when you ask people what they think. In the world of asking, respondents will rub away rough edges to make ideas easier to accept.

So, What Do We Do?

The solution is remarkably simple, but frustratingly hard to do. It all comes back to response and responsibility. We have to differentiate between the words and their meaning. Between what people say and the actions we should take. Rather than worrying about how much or how little people like our ideas, our goal should be to gather together a wide range of responses, both good and bad, and then try to understand why people have responded in the way they have. Whether or not someone likes our idea is not what matters most. We must learn to become appeal agnostic. In a world which worships 'like', that is a hard thing to do.

Ask Yourself Why

To resist the temptation of being beguiled by the popularity of your idea, ask yourself why.

Of course, you need to start by asking your intended audience why. Because if you don't ask, you won't know. But beware. Encouraging your respondents to deconstruct their instinctive response is fraught with danger. Over-considered answers are as likely to be misleading as they are helpful. Expecting someone to know why they like an idea is akin to asking them why they think a joke is funny. We don't always know why something makes us laugh. The solution to understanding the appeal of your idea does not, therefore, necessarily lie with those you are asking. To distinguish between good appeal and bad, ask yourself why. To be more specific, there are five must ask, 'ask yourself why' questions:

1. Do they like my idea because it is familiar and similar to what they already know?

2. Do they like my idea because it makes it easy for them to keep on doing what they currently do?

3. Do they dislike my idea because it challenges the very behaviours and attitudes I am hoping to shift? Or do they dislike my idea because it's actually a bit shit?

4. Are the parts of my idea they reject the rough edges that are going to make my idea stand out? Or do they fundamentally undermine people's ability to engage with the concept?

5. Do people like my idea because they're being nice to me?

Except for the last one (where the answer is probably yes), I cannot answer the questions for you. Every idea is different, every case is unique and there is no silver bullet. All I can do is implore you to recognise how many or how much people like your idea is not a reliable indicator of success or failure. Just because nine out of ten people like your idea does not mean you have a winner. The lone dissenting voice may hold the key to success.

One thing is for sure. If you smooth away the sharp edges that challenge the status quo, make your idea like everything else, and conform to the easy and familiar, you will doom yourself to certain failure.

Judgement Day

It is a point so important it's worth labouring. When you show people your ideas, you are asking them to judge. That is their job. But you don't have to accept their judgement. That is your job. And you cannot do your job properly if you've been seduced by a smiley face.

'Do you like my idea?' is a simple question to ask and an easy question to answer. Yet appeal is not a linear concept. What people like is not always what they should get. The secret to asking people what they think without getting into trouble is to take appeal off its pedestal, to shift the focus from how much or how little they like the idea to understanding why they feel the way they do. Our job is to care less about whether people like the idea and put more effort into asking ourselves why.

If you know how well your idea performs, but you don't know why, you are asking for trouble. You have committed the cardinal sin of allowing yourself to be consumer-led rather than consumer-centred. You've handed the car keys to your respondents and asked them to take you to a destination of their choosing. You need to get back in the driver's seat. Understanding appeal is more important than the appeal itself. Your responsibility greater than their response. To get to grips with the illusion of appeal, ask yourself why.

5

Purpose

What do you think of my idea?
What does it do?
How well does it do it?
What needs does it fulfil?
What are the benefits?

McDonald's was in trouble, and Morgan Spurlock was largely to blame. The *Super Size Me* documentary, directed by and starring Spurlock, had seemingly done irreparable damage to the brand, placing it at the forefront of an obesity epidemic sweeping across the US and beyond. Compounding the problem, a new wave of rivals in the UK were busy demonstrating to the public that fast food could be both tasty and nutritious. Determined to prove their detractors wrong, McDonald's decided to introduce salads, fruit and healthy options onto the menu. Sales continued to decline. The business had lost its way.

Jill McDonald joined McDonald's from British Airways as chief marketing officer and set to work turning the business around. She succeeded – in a supersize me way. McDonald oversaw thirty-seven quarters of continuous growth, despite the changing tastes of UK consumers, a deep recession in the global economy and a turbulent time for the US parent company.[3]

For the newly installed CMO, customer research held the key to success. She said, 'One thing I did when I joined the business was to really dial up the investment in consumer insight. Absolutely number one is to get closer to your customers and get superior insight. That's a real competitive advantage.'

Wise words indeed. But a word of warning. Tempting though it may be to endorse the principle that a greater commitment to customer research has the power to transform the fortunes of a business, in practice, the only thing more asking guarantees is more answers. Volume of response is not necessarily related to value of insight. McDonald's superior understanding, customer closeness and competitive advantage were not achieved through increased investment alone. Something else was going on: There was a pivoting of purpose.

According to McDonald, 'The brand was under attack. From our point of view, *Super Size Me* wasn't a balanced view, but it was a bit of a wake-up call in terms of needing to do better about communicating to consumers the quality of our food and the truth about our food.'

The aim of the research before McDonald's arrival was to understand how to transform the brand to better meet the changing needs of its customers. After her appointment, the primary focus was to learn how best to communicate what made McDonald's great. The renewed commitment to asking people what they thought was only helpful because it was rooted in the brand's true purpose. The brief changed from 'Which of these three healthy options do you prefer?' to 'Which of these creative ideas best brings to life the quality of our burgers?' Instead of asking parents whether their children preferred apples or oranges, the research team went back to asking kids, 'What do you think of these three flavours for our new ice-cream desert?'

The lesson is clear. If you don't know what you stand for when you ask people what they think, it's unlikely you will end up where you want to go. In fact, the reverse is true. The act of asking will just get you to the wrong destination faster.

What Drink Would You Like with Your meal?

Picture the scene: Kendall Jenner drinking a can of Pepsi as she walks through an impassioned mob of protesters. Like her, they are beautiful, youthful, spirited, optimistic and wonderfully diverse. She hands her Pepsi to one of the policemen holding back the angry crowd. Suddenly, the two sides realise they share a common bond – their simi-larities are greater than their differences. They hug. Two warring factions brought to their senses, united over their love of Pepsi.

Pepsi unveil their shiny new ad to the world in great expectation. 'Look at this wonderful statement of togeth-erness,' they seem to be saying, 'an affirmation of mankind with Pepsi at its heart, in touch with a new generation.' What could possibly go wrong?

Then the shit hits the fan. It's an embarrassment. The ad gets pulled. Everyone has to apologise. Even my mother has to apologise. And Pepsi admit, 'We missed the mark, we got it wrong. We're sorry'. For sure, we all make mistakes. The question is, how? How does *that* happen?

The Illusion of Purpose

The trouble was caused by an illusion of purpose.

We live our ideas. The longer we work on an idea, the further removed we become from the people we are trying to convince. That's why we ask people what they think; to stay in touch with reality. Yet paradoxically, the very act of asking brings people into our orbit and closer to our own over-sensitised view of the world. We are in it together. Instantly, when you ask people what they think, you share a vision, you are united. Your respondents embrace your idea as their own, they share your values and ponder how far your brand can stretch. But the togetherness is an illusion, no more real than protesters dancing with policemen in a post-Pepsi state of harmony and bliss.

Collusion not Confirmation

Much is made of the concept of confirmation bias. And of course, hearing what we want to hear is a perennial problem in the world of asking. But right now, we have bigger fish to deep fry. When you ask people what they think, you bring them into your world. As a result, you can stand for anything you want. Together, you can co-create a fantasy. The atmosphere of collusion can be far more dangerous than confirmation bias. McDonald's can become the guardians of a nation's health and Pepsi can bring peace to man and womankind.

When it comes to real life, it's a rather different story. Your idea must have integrity. The same is true for all brands, big and small, old and new. Even in the most well-established and competitive of markets, where the long-term success of the brand relies almost entirely on its ability to connect with consumers through a shared set of emotionally resonant values, there must remain an authentic kernel of truth at the heart of the brand's marketing strategy. And the truth is, Pepsi does not stand for conflict resolution. To make good decisions based on other people's opinions, you must be true to yourself.

Still Hungry?

Harvester is a chain of restaurants offering grilled chicken, burgers, chips and a free, refillable salad bowl taken from the salad cart that sits in the middle of the restaurant. Like McDonald's, Harvester was going through a tough time. Sales were poor and satisfaction scores were low.

When asked why they weren't going as often as they used to, lapsed customers said that, above all, the salad cart put them off. It was terminally disappointing. The choice of salads never changed, there were croutons and bits of coleslaw in the pasta salad, the lettuce was limp, dressing dripped over the side of the cart and the stray pieces of salad that fell on the floor weren't cleared up. The whole thing was a mess.

An unclean salad cart speaks volumes. Instead of proclaiming, 'Come on in and feast on the fruits of the harvest,' it shouts, 'Waste as much as you want. What we sell has little or no value.' A chaotic salad cart declares for all to hear, 'If you think this is messy, can you imagine what the kitchen is like?'

The big problem with Harvester was the salad cart. So, the team initiated a trial of a Harvester without the cart, bringing a bowl of salad to the table with every meal – which made everyone's life much easier, but unfortunately meant customers didn't bother to turn up. Why? Because, although the salad cart was the worst part of the experience, it was one of the fundamental pillars that persuaded people to go to Harvester in the first place. If hungry diners visit a Harvester in the expectation of an endless bowl of salad and grilled chicken, and you take away the salad, then why would they go to Harvester?

Quickly, the management team changed tack. They put in a new, improved salad cart and assigned a member of the service team to keep the salads well stocked and the cart tidy at all times. More serving spoons made it easier for people to help themselves to salad without using their fingers, and the selection included a wider variety of fresher, more interesting, modern ingredients. Instead of suggesting throwaway, the salad cart now demonstrated great value. Rather than representing poor quality, it became a beacon of generosity, freshness and abundance – like a harvest. The brand better met its customers' needs by being true to itself.

But that isn't the end of the Harvester story – not by a long shot. While most of the family were now happy to gorge themselves at Harvester, mums still didn't want to go. There was a subplot. One young mother put it like this:

"Whenever we go to Harvester, I have the chicken breast, but it's always dry or underdone. The chicken is never cooked just right. I have to send it back and then I'm eating my meal on my own after everyone else has finished. I won't go to Harvester anymore. My husband loves it, my kids love it, but I won't go."

The moral of the story is clear. If your purpose in life is chicken and salad, then both the chicken and the salad must be spot on. There's no point keeping the salad cart tidy if the chicken is over or undercooked. And there is no purpose to a family restaurant if the most important member of the family is not happy. If you don't want to fall fowl of the illusion of purpose, your brand must be true to itself, its whole self.

When you ask people what they think of your ideas, imagine yourself as Leonardo DiCaprio in *Inception*. To remain strong in the face of the illusion of purpose, you need a totem; an object dreamers use to distinguish their dreams from reality. That totem is what you do. Hang on to what you do. Cherish what you do. Be true to what you do. It will save you from oblivion.

What's my totem?

Thank you for asking. Personally, I never leave home without a tender cooked chicken breast.

A Summary on Purpose

Understanding purpose is one of the cornerstones of asking people what they think. When you ask people for their opinion, you must ask the questions of purpose:

What needs does my idea fulfil?

What are its benefits?

What could I do better?

It's invaluable insight. The response will help you to refine and shape your idea to better meet the needs of your customers. But if you are not careful, if you don't have a keen sense of what you do and what your brand stands for, you risk becoming deluded about people's perception of your idea and losing sight of what it means to them.

You have to be true to yourself.

When it comes to asking people what they think, you have a choice: whether to be Pepsi Kendall or Chicken Leonardo. Leonardo or Kendall? Kendall or Leonardo? Choose wisely. The future of your brand, your idea, your business, depends on it.

6

Relevance

What do you think of my idea?
How does my idea fit into your life?
What does it mean to you?
Can you relate to it? In what way?

In the run-up to their coverage of the Paralympic Games, Channel 4 launched a Saturday lunchtime programme called *That Paralympics Show*. The idea of the show was to educate the British public about Paralympic sport and begin to build their relationship with Paralympic athletes. The premise was simple. The better informed you were about Paralympic sport and the more you engaged with the athletes' backstory, the more likely it was that you would care about them, root for them, and ultimately, watch their event. *That Paralympics Show* was created to build a bridge between a disinterested and detached public and would-be Paralympic superstars.

The show was groundbreaking, informative, fast-paced and fun, but nobody watched it. The viewing figures suggested *That Paralympics Show* wasn't meeting potential viewers' needs. Seemingly, it lacked relevance. To get to the bottom of why, I led a team of researchers tasked with spending their Saturday lunchtimes in people's homes, observing them as they watched the show.

One occasion stood out. I arrived at the apartment of a group of young guys as they were about to crack open the beers and settle down to watch Manchester United vs Liverpool live on TV. They'd forgotten I was coming. You can imagine how thrilled they were to spend the next hour discussing the whys and wherefores of Paralympic sport instead of enjoying the big game. Clearly, the reason why these lads were not watching *That Paralympics Show* had nothing to do with the qualities of the show itself and everything to do with the fact it wasn't Manchester United vs Liverpool. The entire 'watching people watching the show' exercise was a charade.

When you ask people to focus on an idea, you create an illusion of relevance. They intuitively consider what your idea means to them and the role it could play in their life. By default, your idea becomes disproportionately relevant. Sadly, this newfound meaning has as much connection to real-world relevance as a kickabout in the park has to Barcelona vs Real Madrid. In other words, not very much.

The illusion of relevance causes us to overlook the behavioural context in which people will experience our ideas. Whether it be watching football on a Saturday afternoon, preferring ice-cream to apple slices, avoiding anti-smoking messages or leaning on invisible robots, when you ask people what they think, it's remarkably easy to overlook what they do. But overlook at your peril. In a land teeming with illusions, where words cannot be trusted, actions and behaviours are the only things you can count on. Whilst you can't rely on what people *say*, you can depend on what they *do*.

Doing Right by Nature

The destruction of our natural world is one of the most urgent and perplexing challenges we face as a society. The interconnected issues of climate change, destruction of the rain forests, habitat loss, intensive farming, population growth, pollution and plastic packaging are so complex, and the part we play so small, that the whole thing can feel hopeless. Yet, with the exception of a few crazed politicians and self-interested businessmen perched at the top of the dying tree, most of us recognise the level of threat we currently pose to the planet is not sustainable, and we'd quite like to do something about it. The huge disparity between our expressed desire to resolve the problem and our real-world inaction makes wildlife conservation the ideal place to demonstrate the importance of depending on what people do, over and above what they say.

Here's a question for you on behalf of the RSPB – the Royal
Society for the Protection of Birds. Which of these indigenous
endangered species would you most like to save?

The cute and cuddly dormouse:

The even cuter, but not so cuddly hedgehog:

The majestic, but neither cute nor cuddly hen harrier:

What do you think? Just in case you can't decide, I'm going to give you some helpful information and depressing stats.

British dormice are in trouble. Primarily as a result of the loss of ancient woodland, hedgerow and farmland habitats, over the last seventeen years their population has declined by around forty per cent. Ten million hedgehogs have vanished in the last fifteen years. That figure represents over one third of the entire hedgehog population. The downward trend could at least be partially reversed by the removal of hedgehog-unfriendly garden obstacles and a switch to non-poisonous slug pellets. Hen harriers nest on upland moors, where their diet brings them into conflict with farmers rearing grouse for shooting. It is astonishing to think that the interests of a few well-heeled gentlemen, who get their kicks from shooting at a living target, have pushed this magnificent creature to the edge of extinction.

Which campaign are you most keen to support? Surely, it's got to be the hedgehog. Who wouldn't want to save a hedgehog? Well, possibly the millions of us, me included, who lay artificial grass in the garden, replace the broken fence, pave over the front driveway and do everything we can to get rid of those evil slugs.

Perhaps you'd prefer to save the woodland home of the cute and cuddly dormouse. Or did you, in fact, choose not to protest against the building of a new housing development down the road, in the vain hope that it will provide somewhere affordable for your children to live?

Was it the mighty hen harrier that tickled your fund-raising fancy? After all, birds of prey are an extraordinary and wondrous creation. Or maybe you chose instead to give your hard-earned cash to the Teenage Cancer Trust, rather than save a bird you didn't know existed and won't miss when it's gone.

Ask someone what they think and it's all too easy to be convinced that 'Save the Hedgehog' is a relevant reason to donate to the RSPB. But it is not. The hedgehog may be the most engaging of the three options on offer, but that doesn't make it a good reason to hand over cash to a conservation charity, in order to protect a small and prickly mammal that our actions suggest we care little, if anything, about. The hedgehog is a relevant cause when asked, but our endorsement is largely meaningless. Our actions negate our interest.

So, who was the winner? Who did the RSPB choose as their face for the future: Harold the Hedgehog, Dick the Dormouse or Henrietta the Hen Harrier? And the answer is ... Bob the Red Squirrel.

Rather than waste a limited budget attempting to change the entrenched behaviour of a largely apathetic public, Bob was chosen as the face for a campaign that featured on poster sites located near to and outside the houses of parliament during the run-up to the general election. The aim was to impress upon MPs the importance of including the protection of the countryside within their election manifestos. It was a smart thing to do. MPs make

A VOTE FOR BOB IS A VOTE FOR NATURE. VOTEFORBOB.CO.UK

promises at election time and if you can persuade them to put their name to a manifesto pledge to protect nature, you give yourself a fighting chance to hold them account-able during their term in office. The poster is grounded in the behaviour and beliefs of its intended audience. It is a relevant, constructive and creative way of making a dif-ference. And a very good job Bob did of it too. Well, you can't beat a red squirrel.

Good News

Depending on 'do' is not difficult. Nine times out of ten you already know what people do. Usually, it is the behaviour you are trying to tap into or the problem you are hoping to solve. For example:

- We know that smokers don't engage with smoking cessation communications.

- We know that teenagers in care have haphazard lives and a risky approach to sex.

- We know that people put their everyday needs before nature, despite what they might say.

Take Abdi and DigitAl. The act of asking makes Al instantly relevant. Is that relevance real? No. How do we know? Because the poor awareness of Digital Switchover communications amongst the Somali community is the reason why we are talking to Abdi and his pals in the first place. Irrelevant Al is the problem we have been tasked to tackle. To achieve that goal, we cannot afford to be distracted by the illusion of relevance.

The question to be answered is not, 'Why does Al suddenly become relevant?' but rather, 'Why isn't Al relevant for this audience in the first place? In stark contrast to the instant connection Abdi and his friends felt for Al when asked 'What do you think?', in the real world they simply saw DigitAl as a kid's toy. Al wasn't talking to them, he was talking to their children. Cultural differences meant a cartoon character was never going to be a relevant source of switch-over information. Al didn't stand a chance.

Depend on Do

An idea depends on relevance for its survival. 'What does my idea mean to you?' and 'How does it fit into your life?' are important questions that need to be asked. But disappointingly, there's a downside. The act of asking inevitably makes an idea appear disproportionately relevant. If we do not, therefore, put the answer into the context of our audience's lives, we are likely to be led astray.

People misunderstand 'Depend on do'. They consider grounding their understanding of response in current behaviour to be an admission of defeat, an acceptance that you can't change the status quo. Nothing could be further from the truth. By rooting the response in doing, we equip ourselves to cope with the challenges that lie ahead. It's not about avoiding risk, but about taking the risks that will make a difference. When we ask people what they think, by depending on what they do, we recognise the shiny new relevance of our idea is probably an illusion. We take off the blinkers and the rose-tinted spectacles, leaving us better placed, more focused and more determined to develop compelling ideas that have the potential to succeed in the real rather than the imagined world.

Conversely, if we fail to 'Depend on do', it is perfectly possible the opinions of others will leave us facing the wrong direction, living in a fantasy world with DigitAl as our best mate, spending our weekends watching Paralympic sport on TV, while the descendants of Harold the Hedgehog roam the countryside wearing cleverly worded cigarette packs for slippers. It may not intuitively make sense that the solution to understanding what people think is so intimately wrapped up in what they do, but it is. There is an umbilical cord between the two. What people do is the lifeblood of what they think.

7

Listen Little

'Memory is deceptive because it is
coloured by today's events'

Albert Einstein

Y ou don't have to be Einstein to know that memory
is flawed, but it's easy to forget. Oh, the irony. Over
the years, hundreds of studies by psychologists and
behavioural scientists have identified dozens of cognitive
memory biases, all of which point to the same irrefutable
conclusion: we cannot trust the memories of our behaviour.
If we genuinely did what we think we have done, we'd have
eaten less cake, drunk less gin, smoked less weed, done
more exercise, had more sleep, read more books, worked
more productively and saved a lot more money.

The failure to build the difference between real and imagined behaviour into the way in which we interpret response is an unsurprisingly common cause of asking gone wrong. After all, it's harder to 'Depend on do', if people can't accurately recall what they've done.

The controversial cognitive psychologist Elizabeth Loftus is best known for her work on false memories. Early in her career, Loftus revealed the connection between memory distortion and language. She played videos of car accidents to people and asked them what they remembered seeing. If she asked how fast the cars were going when they 'smashed' into each other, viewers of the video estimated they were going seven miles per hour faster than if she substituted the word 'smashed' for 'hit'. And a week after seeing the video, those asked to estimate the speed of the cars with the word 'smashed' remembered seeing broken glass, even though there was none in the film.[4] Turns out memory is not just unreliable, it's malleable.

Loftus has testified for the defence on many of the most high-profile cases in American legal history, including OJ Simpson, Michael Jackson, and more recently, Harvey Weinstein. Loftus says, 'Police officers' biggest mistake is talking too much. They don't wait and let the witness talk.' More of which anon. For now, what concerns us is this:

- When we ask people for their opinion, we create an illusion of relevance.

- To see through the illusion, we must 'Depend on do'.

- However, we can't always rely on what people say they do because, for all kinds of reasons, they misremember.

- And the way in which we ask only serves to mess up memory even more.

That really is a pain in the ask. If we want to 'Depend on do', we have to find a way to distinguish between unadulterated behaviours and distorted memories. Between what is real and what is not. To answer a question as fundamental as that, we need to turn to God.

Praise the Lord

After nearly 2300 episodes, the weekly religious programme *Songs of Praise* was starting to show signs of old age. So, the BBC commissioned research to investigate how best to reinvigorate religious and ethical broadcasting on TV. A very big question indeed.

To facilitate the conversation, participants were asked to bring to the research session one item from their life that summed up how they felt about God. They arrived with the most extraordinary things. One woman brought a jacket that belonged to her father, who had passed away when she was young. Another brought his keyboard to the discussion; Music was his God. Everything people brought, said and did pointed toward the same insightful conclusion: our religious encounters and ethical dilemmas are not well defined, carefully considered lengthy periods of reflection. They are moments of doing. For example: Do I tell the cashier he has given me the wrong change? Should I hand the sad, alcoholic beggar the £5 note in my wallet because I don't have any coins? Should I give way to that car even though it's a BMW? Is it ever okay to use the disabled toilet? And so on.

Thirty minutes on a Sunday evening dedicated to religious broadcasting is a million miles away from the anarchic and impulsive way in which we experience ethics and morality as part of our daily lives. Rather than feature philosophical discussion and contemplative prayer, the BBC should attempt to capture the fleeting moments of morality that characterise our everyday life. Think thirty-second snippets rather than thirty-minute programmes. *Songs of Praise* was not simply an old-fashioned format, it was an outdated concept founded on a perception of how people behave that no longer represented the lives of the viewing public. The same could be said of the way in which we ask people what they do.

The Search for the Holy Grail

Insight literally means having sight into someone's life. They, their behaviours, even their feelings, are in sight. In the world of asking, the search for insight has long been regarded as the most noble and arduous of quests. Yet this notion of insight as an elusive prize, only to be found by the most devoted of disciples, just doesn't stack up. Since an insight is usually the realisation of something everyday and normal, it's unlikely to be earth-shattering. Insights are not grand. What you're looking for is small and obvious. And because insights are small, they're easy to overlook, like fleeting moments of morality, set aside in the search for something more profound. When it comes to grounding response in what people do, you don't have to plumb the unfathomable depths of their irrational behaviour to reveal some previously undiscovered truth. Far from it. Doing is not about revelation. It's the little things people do that will help you find a way through. If you are finding it hard to 'Depend on do', chances are you are looking for the wrong thing. Think everyday snippets of ordinary life, rather than the exceptional and profound.

Breakfast Time

Shredded Wheat has been part of the cereal aisle since 1893. Over the years, the brand has faced one enduring challenge; it's made entirely of shredded wheat. It looks like shredded wheat, smells like shredded wheat and tastes like shredded wheat. In a cereal aisle brim full of fancy new granolas, fruity mueslis and crunchy nut clusters, it can be hard for the more straight-talking cereals of yester-year to retain their consumer relevance.

What keeps existing customers coming back for more is that Shredded Wheat is amazingly good for you. And not just good for your digestive system, but good for your heart as well. That's why it's still around. So, when Cereal Partners tested new ideas based on the concept of Shredded Wheat being good for your heart, you can see how they ended up with the idea, 'i heart Shredded Wheat'.

®

This is the research conversation leading directly to the design that adorned the brand until its most recent refresh.

'What do you think of Shredded Wheat?'
'I eat it occasionally, but I seem to buy other cereals more often.'
'Did you know it's good for your heart?'
'No. I didn't know that.'
'Is your heart important to you?'

'Yes, of course.'

'Are you interested in the concept of a breakfast cereal that is good for your heart?'

'Yes. I'm certainly open to the idea.'

'Which of these three ideas do you prefer?'

'The one with the little "i" and heart-shaped bowl.'

'Why?'

'It tells me something I didn't know, in a way that is creative, modern and inviting.'

The design is unquestionably purposeful, eye-catching and fun. Yet there is another way to approach the same conversation that starts with behaviour and could lead you in a completely different direction. It goes like this:

'Do you buy breakfast cereals for the good of your heart?'

'No. I buy healthy cereals, but not ones that are specifically good for my heart.'

'Why are healthy cereals important to you?'

'They kick-start my day and keep me going till lunch without snacking.'

'Which of these designs do you like the most?'

'Since you're asking, the one with the little "i" and the heart-shaped bowl.'

'Why?'

'It tells me something I didn't know, in a way that is creative, modern and inviting.'

'Are you concerned about the health of your heart?' and 'Do you buy cereals for the good of your heart?' are two entirely different questions. In this instance, whichever approach you take to asking, the preferred design is the same. But if you ground the conversation in the context of prospective customers' cereal buying behaviour, you get a very different impression of the potential relevance of the healthy heart proposition. Your focus might turn instead to the concepts of kick-start or sustenance.

During one of the many research sessions spent testing a variety of 'good for your heart' designs, a helpful mum said the following: 'I have two teenage sons and both of them eat a bowl of Shredded Wheat before they play football, because they think it makes them perform better for longer. In my house, Shredded Wheat is football food.'

Eureka! Now that's what I call an insight.

I'm not sure why the concept of 'Football food' made such an impression on me, but it did. Maybe it's because when I was young, Shredded Wheat advertising featured the biggest cricket star of the day. The sporting insight chimed with my own memories of the brand. Or perhaps, it is because, as I watch my own boys eat unfeasibly large amounts of Weetabix before they play football, I can't help but wonder, what if? Either way, the brilliant simplicity of the 'Football food' insight has been a constant and faithful reminder of an invaluable lesson:

When you ask people what they think of your ideas, if you listen little, their behaviour will reveal itself to you during the course of the conversation. Often, you won't even need to ask. The little things people do will help you overcome the illusion of relevance and provide the solution to the problem you are trying to resolve. The insights you seek are not grand, they're not big and they're not even clever. If you want to enhance the relevance of your idea, start with what people do, and listen little. Simple really.

Beginning and Ending With 'Do'

I want to briefly share with you a salutary tale of 'doing', and then we'll move on.

The UK CEO of a global travel group had a vision for a new type of retail experience. Aimed squarely at high net-worth individuals working in the City of London, the idea was to create a space where the wealthy could indulge their insatiable appetite for adventure. Through inspiring initiatives, state of the art technology and unparalleled levels of service, the ambition was to create a radically different experience to the traditional travel agent, fast disappearing from our high streets.

I spent two weeks talking to lawyers and bankers about how best to realise this vision, exploring what it would take to make the concept distinctive and compelling.

Being a passion project, the CEO was at the debrief, along with a team of marketeers, product managers and designers, all tasked with delivering the new experience.

Armed with a fifty-page PowerPoint presentation, I began by explaining that it was rare for the intended audience to leave the office at lunchtime. Furthermore, their need for a personalised adventure shopping experience was currently well catered for by trusted travel experts with whom they communicated via email and phone. And finally, most of their holidays were booked by their partners and PAs.

At which point, the chief exec stood up, turned to his team and announced, 'We're not doing this'. Then he walked over to me, shook my hand warmly, saying, 'Thank you very much, you've saved us a lot of money.' And left.

Five minutes is all it took.

In twenty-five years, that remains a one-off experience. Nobody else, before nor since, has abandoned ship after five minutes. Normally, the focus is on the following forty-nine pages of the debrief, rather than the opening one. Learning from the CEO, we shouldn't only start with 'do', we should end with it as well.

Relevant Final Thoughts

Understanding relevance is a fundamental reason for asking. If your idea isn't relevant, it cannot succeed. Thankfully, since it is only natural for people to consider how your idea would fit into their lives, relevance will almost certainly be baked into their response. The hard part is working out whether that relevance is real.

The solution is straightforward.

It is your responsibility to reframe the response in the context of your audience's lives – to think about what people do and then work out the extent to which their actions are reflected in their response. Most of the time, the task should not be taxing. Nine times out of ten you already know what people do. It is the problem you are trying to resolve or the behaviour you are attempting to change. For example, food lovers are reluctant to sacrifice flavour for health, and people are unwilling to make compromises today for the sake of the natural world tomorrow.

Depending on 'do' enables you to realistically assess how well your idea meets the needs of your prospective customers and puts you in a better place to make wise decisions as a result. Depending on 'do' sets you on the right path, keeps you on the straight and narrow, and enables you to course correct. Alternatively, if you don't 'Depend on do', and you choose instead to trust what people say, you're asking for trouble.

On those occasions when you don't know what your audience does, it becomes incumbent upon you to find out. By listening little, what people do should reveal itself to you during the course of the conversation. It's unlikely to be a grand revelation. More probably, it will be the realisation of something small, ordinary and everyday. The little things people do will help you find a way through.

8

Impact

What do you think of my idea?
Does it stand out?
Is it distinctive?
Does it grab you?

There's a mighty chasm between impact in the real world and impact in the world of asking. When we ask people what they think of our ideas, no effort is required to stand out. Impact is easy and assured. In the real world, life is tough. The competition grows ever fiercer, our choices continue to expand exponentially and audiences become ever more distracted. Time and time again, ideas that succeed in research fail to live up to expectation because, in a competitive context, they do not cut through. Many of the ideas that burn most brightly at first soon lose their lustre when starved of the money, time, presence and persistence required to fulfil their potential.

Getting Hungry?

It has been at least five minutes since we talked about food and I'm getting hungry, but I'm busy and I don't have time to cook. If like me, you enjoy good, tasty food, but need cooking to be easy and convenient, then I'm interested in your opinion. Which of these packaging designs for a new brand of gourmet frozen ready meals do you prefer?

Pack A

Pack B

The product inside is the same, yet the packs create a radically different impression. Which do you instinctively like more? Which one has the greatest impact? Which one jumps out at you and shouts, 'Buy me!'? The answer is easy. Pack A is definitely classier, but B stands out more.

Here's a different type of question for you: When was the last time you bought a premium frozen ready meal at your local supermarket? The answer is probably never. Frozen peas, chips and ice cream, yes. But a frozen ready meal on the way home from work? No. Come to think of it, why would you even go to the frozen section to buy a ready meal in the first place? It's frozen.

When you ask people, 'What do you think?' the preferences they express are real. They genuinely do think the pretty box is prettier and the bold box stands out more. But what difference does that make? The name, the logo, the design, the packaging, the calorie content and the description of the food are irrelevant if your product is not top of mind and your potential audience is nowhere to be seen. If you ask people what they think of the two packs, it's a beauty parade. Impact in the world of asking becomes a question of fonts and colours. If you think beyond the instinctive response and consider the wider context in which your prospective customers will experience your idea, impact involves a frenetic fight for headspace and demands a dramatic change in consumer behaviour. That is a whole different ball game.

The Illusion of Impact

Asking people what they think gives the impression that impact is a two-dimensional concept:

Does my idea appear different?

Will it stand out?

But there's more to impact than being seen and heard. The illusion of impact narrows our view of the world in which our ideas are going to live and causes us to underestimate the scale of the job to be done. That is the trouble with asking. When we ask people for their opinions, we become isolated from the challenges that lie ahead. It's a ready meal recipe for disaster.

Let Them Eat (Frozen) Cake

In 1997, frozen cake salesman Ed Perry joined forces with his favourite client, talented Chef Dale Penfold, to open a small shop selling hand-prepared, savoury frozen meals. The shop was called 'Cook'. Their dream was to be the world's best-ever maker of frozen ready meals.

Twenty-three years on, Cook has over ninety shops throughout the UK. Alongside this commitment to their own retail presence, dedicated Cook freezer cabinets have also appeared at the front of local supermarkets across the land. Ed and Dale understood that getting people to buy frozen ready meals involved more than making appetising products and the development of a compelling brand. If their consumers were not in the right part of the store and frozen ready meals were not top of mind, having an enticing offer and distinctive packaging was never going to be enough.

Boxed was launched in March 2018 to compete for a slice of the growing market for premium ready meals. The packaging was attractive and the product was good. Yet, starved of the front-of-mind awareness and front-of-store presence on which its existence depended, Boxed struggled to survive.

The lesson could not be clearer: Asked-for impact is about noise and colour. Real-world impact has more depth. Success relies on our ability to force ourselves into the lives of our consumers and sustain that engagement over time. It's not just about being noticed on day one, but about building a connection with your consumers on days two, three, four, five and beyond. It's easy to think of impact as a moment in time. Have I got your attention? Have you noticed how distinctive I am? But the story of your idea doesn't stop once you've been spotted. Realising your ambitions relies on an ongoing interaction between your customers and your idea.

What are the implications for the way in which we interpret response?

Up to this point, to address the troublesome biases and distortions that result from asking people what they think, we have had to concentrate on putting the response

into the context of what people currently do. Our gaze
has been firmly fixed on the present. Getting to grips with
the illusion of impact demands a slightly different approach.
To get a true sense of the scale of the challenge that awaits
us, we must look to the future. It is our job to envisage
the competitive reality in which our idea is going to fight
for survival, and hopefully, thrive.

Paths to Glory

Before we get going, you should know that travelling to the
future is not a task for the faint of heart. In a distracted,
noisy world, successful brands and services are engaged in
a constant and relentless struggle to attract attention and
stay top of mind. An endless stream of competitors, young
and old, are waiting to take us down. There is a reason why
a programme of marketing is called a campaign. It's because
we are waging war. Market surveillance and scouting mis-
sions are a critical part of any successful programme of
development, but an unplanned foray into enemy territory,
all guns blazing, is not a brave attack; it's a suicide mission.
We don't ask people what they think of our ideas because
we want to work out the best way to commit Hara-Kiri.

Our purpose is to prepare for battle.

We are the SWOT team. Our assignment is to analyse
strengths, spot weaknesses, investigate opportunities and
assess the level of threat. To meet our objectives, the

interrogation of our prospective customers must go way beyond stand out. These are the questions we need to ask:

What weapons do we have at our disposal?

What is our Achilles heel?

How committed are prospective customers to their current behaviours?

How high are their barriers to participation and engagement?

What is our best plan of attack? When are the market leaders at their most vulnerable?

How can we protect our gains in the face of an inevitable competitor backlash?

What do we need to do to cut through, stay strong, keep fighting and win the war?

Although we are planning a strategy for the battle ahead, the questions we ask our potential consumers are still firmly fixed in the here and now. Why? Because if we prompt our respondents to predict how they might engage with our ideas in the future, we are, in effect, encouraging them to make stuff up. Giving people the licence to create a fantasy world founded on an illusion of interest is asking for double trouble. Readying yourself for the future is not about prediction and fantasy, it's about asking the right questions. And those questions are always rooted in the present. Ask about the present, think about the future.

Making an Impact

Make no mistake; it's tough out there. There are 30,000 consumer products launched in the US each year. In the UK, publishers release more than twenty new book titles every hour. Over 13,000 restaurants were launched in the US in 2018. Between 2016 and 2018, 6,140 mobile apps were released through the Google Play Store every day. You get the point.

An army marches on its stomach. Asking about stand-out and distinctiveness is merely a light starter. Being well-provisioned for the challenges that lie ahead requires a more rounded, robust diet of competitor and consumer insight, frozen or otherwise. The information we gather about our prospective audience's likes, needs, habits and motivations will define our strategy, sustain us through the conflict and lead us to glory. To combat the illusion of impact, prepare for battle.

9

Clarity

What do you think of my idea?
Is it clear?
Do you understand it?

Populist politicians across the globe have grabbed
hold of the reins of power through the smart use
of simple three or four-word slogans. The clarity of
the message seemingly attracts huge popular support, no
matter how vacuous and meaningless the underlying policy
may be.

In commerce, clarity carries equal weight. Whether it
be Apple, Amazon, Google, Netflix, Facebook, Instagram
Twitter or WhatsApp, the user experience and the brand
identity of the tech companies that now dominate our
lives are defined by their simplicity.

Given its potential to unlock the doors to power and wealth, it is hardly surprising that clarity is among the most important and productive reasons for asking people what they think. We are too close to our own ideas to know whether or not they are clear. What is simple and obvious to us may be confusing and obscure to others. Without asking, we would never know. By far and away the most common criticism I've heard over the last twenty years is that the concept being tested is unclear. Most ideas start off over-complicated and asking people what they think helps us strip back and simplify.

In theory, the question of clarity should be clear cut. An idea is either clear or it is not. Your audience either gets the message or they don't. The benefits of your product are either obvious or they're not. Your website's navigation is either intuitive or it is not. And so on. In practice, things are rarely so straightforward. When we ask people what they think, we regularly do two things to muddy the waters:

1. We wait for the penny to drop

2. We talk too much

Since both causes of the illusion of clarity are problems of our own making, it seems sensible to spend a bit of time clearing them up. Like all cleaning jobs, it is an essential task. No matter how hard you search, in murky waters you will never be able to find the keys to success.

Letting the Penny Drop

The following two phrases are designed to encourage people to support an additional tax on the tobacco industry.[5]

1. The tobacco levy is a charge on tobacco companies' profits that would be used to fund the NHS.
   Support the Tobacco Levy

2. The tobacco industry causes harm to people's health and society as a whole.
   They should pay to fix the harm they cause.
   Support the Tobacco Levy

When shown the statements, respondents read each phrase, pause, then reread them, this time more slowly. Some even read the messages a third time. Finally, the penny drops. And with the meaning now clear in their minds, they feel free to give their opinion. Something about both phrases makes them difficult for the reader to take on board at the first time of asking. Yet, there's nothing about either statement that is inherently difficult to understand. For some strange reason, it just takes a bit of time for people to get the message straight in their heads.

Thankfully, in the world of asking, participants are happy to read and reread the lines until the penny drops. In the real world, that's not how people operate. They either get an idea or they don't. Nobody, but nobody is going to take the time, nor make the effort, to decipher a message they don't immediately understand.

First Things First

Making good decisions relies on our ability to focus on what is important. If the people we are asking don't understand our idea straight away, then it becomes our chief responsibility to work out why.

Whatever our original reasons for asking, resolving clarity becomes our top priority.

Using the tobacco levy lines as an example, the initial brief was to work out which of the concepts was more compelling – a levy on profit or payment for harm caused. As soon as we asked, our mission changed. Our primary concern became answering the questions of clarity:

Why did it take so long for the penny to drop?

Why did people have to read each message twice?

Why did the words take so long to sink in?

What got in the way?

And by changing the mission, all became clear. The problem with both messages was the word 'levy'. It's a terrible word. What is a levy? How does it work? Who pays? What is the difference between a levy and a tax? Why is there a Chevy in the Levy? I don't know. It makes no sense. Both phrases were fine. It was the lack of clarity surrounding the word 'levy' that was getting in the way.

But the fun didn't stop there. By asking people to read the messages aloud, we gained a real insight into the true nature of the problem. They read the word 'levy' as 'Levi', as in Levi's jeans. Which explains why the message didn't sink in. Tobacco trousers makes no sense at all. Although, to be fair, if smokers were addicted to denim instead of cigarettes, it might significantly ease the burden on our overstretched health service.

That aside, the implications were clear. Rather than worrying about which of the phrases was more engaging, the language of levy needed to be sorted out.

When we ask people what they think, we must be on constant alert for the signs and signals of penny dropping. Rereads, furrowed brows, delayed responses and whirring cogs are all strong indicators that something is not right. If there is even the slightest hint of a lack of clarity, we have to find out why. Because until we crack clarity, we cannot move on.

Talking Too Much

What do you think of this urgent and important rallying cry for the World Wildlife Fund?

**Our planet needs your support now.
More than ever. Join WWF.**

Typically, the response is, 'The planet definitely needs our support, but I'm not clear what that's got to do with WWF.' Let me explain. If you think about it, saving tigers relies on protecting their habitat. WWF works with local communities, businesses and governments to ensure that people and animals can coexist in harmony. You might automatically associate WWF with endangered species, but it is, in fact, the world's leading independent conservation organisation. Join WWF and help save the planet.

'I hadn't thought of WWF like that,' comes the reply. 'Thank you for explaining. Now I have a clearer understanding of the wider role of the WWF, the charity has become more relevant. When I think about it, giving to WWF to protect the planet doesn't just make sense, it's a damn good idea.'

Given the opportunity to explain, everything and anything becomes clear. But in the real world, you don't get the chance. Clarity is immediate. An idea is either clear or it is not. The aim of asking is to check for clarity, and yet the way we frame and explain our ideas often creates the false impression that all is clear when it is not. The trouble is we talk too much. Most of the time, we set up and explain our ideas in a way that gives the game away. We put the idea into context, reveal its purpose and point out the benefits. And then, if people are still struggling, we describe the idea to them in more detail. Rarely do we have the confidence to just ask. To let our ideas be.

When asking for opinions, our inclination is to focus on how well an idea performs. Consequently, we set up and explain the idea in order to allow people to judge how good it is. If we cared more about meaning and less about performance, there'd be a lot less talk and a lot more listening. When it comes to asking, there is one golden rule that takes precedence over all others:

Telling is selling.

If you need to frame, explain or justify your idea, you're not asking, you're selling. You've abandoned your quest for understanding in favour of a sale of goods or services. Telling is selling. That is our three-word slogan. It's a winner. I've even got the caps printed. I'm not joking. I really have.

To avoid the trap of selling when you ask people what they think, my advice is this: keep it simple. Say as little as you can. Do not give the game away. Should you need to describe your idea to someone, only tell them what they could and would know if they came across the idea in the real world. Anything else is extra. Whatever information you provide that relies on you being there to explain is unrealistic, unnecessary and unwelcome.

If those you are asking don't get your idea immediately, the only solution is to go back to the drawing board and find a way of asking that doesn't require an explanation. It's a good exercise. Because if you can't make your idea clear when you ask people what they think, it sure as hell won't be clear in the real world.

Clearing Things Up

Clarity could never claim to be the most exciting wonder of the world of asking. Appeal is always going to win that contest. But in many ways, clarity is more important. Your idea cannot be appealing, relevant, purposeful, impactful, believable, personable or desirable if people don't get it.

To properly understand the clarity of your idea, you should keep the asking simple. If it takes time for the penny to drop, you need to find out why. Your primary task is to understand how you can remove the barriers that inhibit clarity and comprehension. If you set up, describe or explain your idea in a way that clarifies its purpose, values or meaning, you are asking for trouble. Let your idea do the talking.

10

Belief

What do you think of my idea?
Is it credible?
Would you rely on it?

We're on our way to Worcester, a fine city in the heart of the English countryside. Abdi promises to smoke out of the window and Finn is exceptionally good company. Come with us. You can drive if you want. The team responsible for the communication of government environmental policy want to know what the good country folk of Worcester think about the following two policy statements:[6]

1. The government believes a cleaner environment benefits people and the economy.

2. The government is delivering a cleaner environment for the next generation.

The question to be answered is this: Do the people of Worcester want environmental policy to focus on economic benefits or future generations?

Here are the results:
Policy Statement One: A healthy economy **33%**
Policy Statement Two: A healthy future for our kids **67%**.

The outcome is clear. Communications should prioritise protecting the planet for our children, over and above the benefits to the economy. That is broadly what you'd expect. While the economy wins elections, the well-being of future generations tends to triumph in policy beauty contests. However, if you'd joined us on the streets of Worcester, you'd know the instinctive answers had little if anything to do with the relative merits of either statement. The reflex response of ninety-five per cent of the people asked was, 'It's all bullshit. I don't believe a word of it.'

The coronation of Policy Statement Two is a sham. When it comes to environmental promises, nobody believes anything the government says anyway. Sixty-seven per cent is a good score, but sixty-seven per cent of zero is still zero. The result is an illusion. Neither phrase is believable.

Implied Credibility

There are two aspects to the illusion of belief. Firstly, the act of asking tends to bestow credibility upon an idea. By implication, an idea that is good enough to be presented must also be worthy of belief. Like the policy statements tested on the streets of Worcester, that may not be the case. The way to cope with the threat of implied credibility is to create an environment for asking in which people feel free to express their instinctive feelings openly, honestly and without reservation. The Good Asking Guide provides advice on how best to achieve that goal.

The second aspect to the illusion of belief is more subtle, and therefore, far more dangerous.

The Importance of Proof

'What do you think of this idea?' is a rational question. It's a straightforward request to think things through. You can change how you ask the question from 'What do you *think* of the idea? to 'How do you *feel* about the idea?', but you're not fooling anyone. People are not stupid. However you choose to frame the question, they know they have been asked to focus on an idea and give their considered opinion. Asking encourages those being asked to use their heads rather than their hearts. In stark contrast to the unconscious, irrational drivers of behaviour in the real world, rational response dominates in the thoughtful world of asking. This dramatic shift in emphasis from emotional to rational thinking has an important consequence: Asking for opinions artificially promotes the importance of proof.

When we show people our ideas, the rational research environment prompts them to request facts and further information. But they don't really need facts. If the people you are asking don't intuitively believe your idea, it is because your idea is not believable. The need for proof is a trick. And I'll prove it. Well, Sarah and Rob will, anyway.

Sarah and Rob

Sarah and Rob are morbidly obese. Rob has had a gastric bypass and suffers from type 2 diabetes. Both have problems with their joints and find walking difficult. People are quick to judge the obviously overweight, and life for Sarah and Rob can be challenging and unpleasant. Sarah, in particular, endures shocking levels of abuse. Most poignantly, Sarah and Rob desperately want a child, but Sarah is having trouble conceiving. She has been told by doctors her size is the main reason she can't get pregnant. Recently, she has been denied access to fertility treatment because of her weight. Sarah and Rob are heartbroken.

What can you tell the two of them about the consequences of obesity that they don't already know? There is no more powerful driver in Sarah and Rob's personal battle with weight-loss than childlessness. Their knowledge of the consequences of obesity goes way beyond the warnings of medical professionals and well-intentioned public health campaigns. Sarah and Rob live the consequences.

And yet, when shown concepts highlighting the link between obesity and cancer, the first thing they ask for is proof. 'Show me the facts,' they demand. 'How can I believe it when I don't have the facts? Prove it!'

It doesn't make sense. Sarah and Rob cannot possibly be interested in learning more about the dangers of obesity. So why would they ask for facts? The reason is simple. Their requests for proof and further information are a get-out clause. Far from being a question of belief, asking for proof is an easy and effective way of saying, 'I'm not prepared to take on board what you are showing me or listen to what you have to say.' Sarah and Rob's need for proof is an illusion. Their requests and demands are a masquerade. The need for proof is nothing more than rejection and resistance in disguise.

More of what Sarah and Rob have historically chosen to ignore is not miraculously going to make them more interested. Actually, the reverse is true. Facts are dull and evidence is boring. Both are the preserve of those who are already engaged and the most positively predisposed.

Feelings Before Facts

Belief is an important yet oft-overlooked wonder of the world of asking. We need to know whether our potential customers think our message is credible and our product worthy of their trust. But more proof is rarely if ever the solution. In the real world, trust, faith and credence are emotional concepts underpinned by genuine experience. Only in the world of asking is belief overtly rational. As a result, facts and further information become inordinately important. But the need for proof is an illusion. The constant demands for evidence and reasons to believe are nothing more than a distraction. When you ask people for their opinion, there are only four facts you need to know:

1. Requests for evidence and further information are sure signs of resistance and rejection in disguise.

2. Your product is your proof. If those you are asking don't believe your idea without proof, then your idea is not believable.

3. If your researcher recommends the key to success is proof points and supporting evidence, it's time to get a new researcher.

4. If you work in marketing and find yourself believing your consumers need facts and stats, you should move to accounts, spend more time with excel spreadsheets, and leave the fun bit to someone who knows what they are doing.

11

Personality

What do you think of my idea?
How does it come across?
What words would you use to describe it?
What are its values?
Do you like my style?

Every thing has a personality. Whether it be the laptop on which our working life depends or the coffee cup in our kitchen cupboard, the personality of a thing is part of what makes it unique. Apple has a different personality to Microsoft, Samsung to Sony, Nike to Adidas, Starbucks to Costa, and Crunchy Nut Cornflakes to Coco Pops. It is through our personality that we convey how we want to be seen by the world. From product design to brand identity and from marketing communications to customer experience, every facet of an idea contributes to the development of a healthy and robust personality.

Our personality elevates our idea above its functional purpose. It determines the relationship people have with our idea, not simply for what it does, but for the person it is. If it were a person, of course.

In the words of Walt Disney:

> *'Until a character becomes a personality it cannot be believed. And without personality a story cannot ring true to the audience.'*

Story Time

Long long ago, in the faraway land of hopes and dreams, a little-known animator called Nick Park won an Academy Award for a five-minute claymation mockumentary called *Creature Comforts.*[7]

Two stars of the advertising industry, Phil Rylance and Paul Cardwell, saw *Creature Comforts* and were convinced that, if they could capture the charm of the original film, it could form the basis for a great advertising campaign. Together with Nick Park, they created a magical series of adverts for the erstwhile Electricity Board. Each ad featured an entertaining 30-second vignette of a clay animal enjoying the benefits of their new electrical appliance. They included a tortoise describing the joy of returning to a warm flat after a freezing ten-mile run and a family of penguins extolling the virtues of their new electric cooker with a ceramic hob. The advertising became part of the fabric of the nation, phrases from the commercials entered the vernacular and the characters themselves were adopted as much-loved national treasures.

I launched my first research company around the same time, and partly due to the success of *Creature Comforts*, my colleagues and I have been testing marketing ideas featuring animated characters ever since. Whatever the subject matter, be it tax, tissues, banks, butter, car tyres or a cup of tea: you name it, it's been cartooned.

When you ask people what they think, the enthusiasm for animated advertising concepts knows no bounds. Respondents instantly adore the characters. They embrace their quirky features and fall in love with their cheeky personalities. They bring the animated characters to life in their minds, creating imaginary family units and meaningful backstories. They recognise the potential for their relationship with the cartoons to grow and develop over time. Most importantly, they acknowledge that their love for the characters will help them to forge stronger, deeper ties with the brand they so cleverly intend to promote. Just like *Creature Comforts*.

It's such a shame the response is an illusion – no more real than the characters themselves. In the real world, you can't begin to recreate the same deep connection people have with your idea when you ask them what they think. The subtle details that seem to have such an impact on those you are asking may not even register when people come across your idea amid their busy lives. There's little or no time for meaningful conversation or a chance to get to know each other better. In the real world, building a compelling personality takes a tad more effort and a lot more cash.

A Love Story

Our ideas are our babies. We conceive them, nurture them, invest in them and love them. To us, their personalities are complex, multi-layered and richly textured. When we ask our potential customers what they think, we want to know they feel the same way. So, to facilitate the conversation about personality, we help our respondents along. In questionnaires, we give people a list of adjectives to pick from. Which of these words best describes how you feel about the personality of this idea: Youthful, energetic, clever, fun, friendly, kind, trustworthy, proud, sociable or serious? In qualitative research, we play games called projective techniques, designed to personify our ideas, literally.

> If the idea was one of your friends or relatives, which one would it be and why?
> If the idea was at a party, would it sit quietly in the corner sipping a glass of squash, chat happily over a shared bottle of chardonnay, or drink too many strawberry mojitos and dance half-naked on the kitchen table?

Like any parent, we lap it up. We love to hear people talking about the personality of our ideas. In doing so, we lose the ability to separate fact from fiction. Remember the house of mirrors. Looking longingly into the mirror of personality, it is especially easy to forget the image staring back at us is an overblown fantasy. When we ask people what they think, we must decide – whether we wish to build a connection with our customers based on a caricature of our real selves, or to develop a relationship based on a personality of substance.

They're Back!

Many years later, *Creature Comforts* made a comeback – in a different guise – for a charity called Leonard Cheshire Disability. This time, the campaign was called *Creature Discomforts* and featured six animal characters, each with a disability. The aim was to raise awareness about the lives and experiences of disabled people, in their own words.

In research groups, *Creature Discomforts* went down a storm. Of course respondents enjoyed the cute cartoons, but of more significance was the role each character played in the communication of the core message. Flash the Sausage Dog and Peg the Hedgehog enabled people to engage in a conversation about disability they would otherwise have been unwilling to have. Importantly, the charm of the creatures encouraged the audience to consider their own attitudes and behaviours towards disabled people, without becoming defensive. Seemingly, a cartoon character in a wheelchair can teach the public what it feels like to be overlooked and ignored in a way that a real person simply cannot. The characters had a purpose. Their personalities were integral to the story being told.

The campaign achieved extraordinary media coverage on a shoestring budget. Fifty-one per cent of all adults recalled both the advertising and its messages. Likeability scores for the animations were at seventy-five per cent – exceptionally high for an 'unappealing' subject such as disability. Significantly, a third of people admitted they had more to learn about disability, and the marketing team at Leonard Cheshire received an unprecedented level of engagement and feedback from people who wished to use the *Creature Discomforts* adverts for training and education purposes.[8]

Yet with limited exposure, the public never had the opportunity to become acquainted with the finer details of Peg the hedgehog's personality in the same way as they had with the original family of penguins and their fancy ceramic hob. Their engagement with the concept was not determined by the cuteness of the characters. The success of *Creature Discomforts* was down to the integrity of the idea. There was an authentic and coherent connection between the purpose of the advertising and its personality. Like all great campaigns, the 'why' was joined at the hip with the 'who'.

A Story of Substance

The illusion of personality has two faces:

1. The act of asking overstates the depth of an idea's personality. People see and connect with stuff they wouldn't normally notice.

2. The world of asking is a place where the superficial can thrive.

Time and time again, manufactured marketing concepts based on borrowed personalities perform well in consumer research. And why wouldn't they? After all, it doesn't matter whether an idea has substance because the world of asking is a land of make-believe. You can be who you want to be and say what you want to say. Personalities can be moulded in an instant. Artificial traits and characteristics can be bolted on. Relationships can blossom and grow in seconds. Through the asking, we can superimpose a brand story upon our captive audience, which can be neither substantiated nor sustained. The real world is different. Only the sincere will survive.

The solution, as ever, is to behave responsibly. Asking your audience about the style and tone of your idea is an important exercise, but as a responsible parent, you cannot afford to get carried away. Over-indulgence will only result in a spoilt idea. Keep your conversations about personality simple and steer clear of the superficial. Use the asking to help you develop a personality that rings true to your audience, not only in the animated world of asking, but in the living breathing world as well. As you watch your idea develop into a strapping young business or a fine marketing concept, you'll derive great satisfaction from the rock-solid connection between what your idea does and the person it is. If it were a person, of course.

Stumped

That's it. The Wonder Wheel has turned full circle and we're back at appeal. And what a lovely surprise. Just like the first time around, our friends the *Superhumans* are here to greet us. But this time something is different. Maybe it's the colour, noise and sounds of Rio 2016 that makes everything seem so strange. No. There's more to it than that. Their personality has changed.

Based on the success of *Superhumans 2012*, the team at Channel 4 came up with a new expression of the campaign for the 2016 games that was equally as powerful as the original. The idea was to cross out the 'dis' in disability and focus instead on ability. The internal working title for the new campaign was *Fuck Dis*, and the initial creative concept featured a series of vignettes which challenged perceptions of what it was possible for people with disability to achieve. The scripts that went into research were strong, confident and didn't hold back. Just like 2012.

The appeal of the idea was mixed. Respondents understood why Channel 4 would want the new *Superhumans* campaign to retain the personality of the iconic advertising that had such a dramatic impact on them four years ago. But the world had moved on. 2012 had forced people to rethink their attitudes toward Paralympic athletes and the combative, strident tone of voice no longer felt appropriate. It was time for the *Superhumans* to show the softer side of their personality.

Conceptually, the launch advertising for Channel 4's coverage of the Rio 2016 Paralympic Games was almost identical to the script shown in research. It was still underpinned by the concept of ability rather than disability, but now, the ad was built around the phrase 'Yes you can!' and the forceful tone had been replaced by a personality of relentless positivity. The result was extraordinary. You should watch it on YouTube. The ad is one of the most uplifting, emotionally engaging pieces of communication you will ever see.[9] I guarantee you'll love it.

But that's not where the story ends.

When the scripts were tested in research, something other than the overly assertive tone of voice wasn't quite right. The strength of connection with the idea was lacking. Respondents were not as engaged as they had been in 2012, for good or for bad. And it was hard to put your finger on why. Then, as had been the case first time around, one person expressed an opinion that made everything fall into place. The lone voice said this:

"I know it's not right, but stumps always make me feel uncomfortable. It would be easier to watch if there weren't so many stumps on show."

It was a reservation as honest as it was revealing. The images being used to bring the script to life included numerous pictures of Paralympians with their stumps showing. Much the same as the image of the black and white cat I met on my first day of asking all those years ago, an uncomfortable visual truth was provoking people to disconnect from the cause. At that moment, it was clear what had to be done. Like 2012, part of what made the concept difficult to like in research became an essential component of the final commercial. If you watch the ad, you'll see a lot of stumps. Deliberately.

And so, as our passage around the outer ring of the Wonder Wheel draws to a close, we end with the same simple moral as we started: appeal is not a straightforward concept, and what people wish for in the world of asking is not always what they should get.

12

Desire

What do you think of my idea?
Are you interested?
Do you want it?

The question of desire comes in many different guises:

Would you download the app?
Would you share the idea on Facebook?
Would you click on the link to find out more?
Would you take part?
Would you sign up?
Would you donate to the cause?
Would the idea make you change your ways?
Would you buy it?

Often, asking about desire is couched in more subtle terms:

> How motivating is my idea?
>
> How compelling?
>
> How engaging?
>
> Does it change your perception of the brand?
>
> Does it make my idea more enticing?

The answer when we ask is almost certainly yes. The reality is more likely to be no.

Asking people what they think of an idea sets up the perfect sale. The people being asked focus on the idea in question. They contemplate its pros and cons. They seek out its purpose. They consider how it could and would fit into their lives. Impact is assured. They take the time to work through any areas of uncertainty and confusion. They listen attentively as the most convincing benefits are explained. Facts and further information support their newfound faith. And finally, they hone in on the subtle details that define the personality of the idea, that give it life. Then we ask, 'Are you interested? Are you motivated? Do you want my idea?'

No commitment is required. No money changes hands. There's no pressure. All they have to do is say yes. It is the perfect imaginary sale, the greatest and the grandest illusion of them all. As the parent or promoter of an idea, it is so compelling to hear people telling us how much they like and want our baby that we quickly become divorced from reality. It's only natural to get over-excited when someone says, 'I want your idea.' But it's a delusion. Don't get dizzy. Chances are, real commitment is a fantasy.

Free Love

During conversations about ideas, people often volunteer expressions of desire without prompting. For example:

> 'I'm very interested. When will it be available to buy?'
> 'The advert is a good trigger to check out the website.'
> 'That is so useful. I wish I could take it home now.'

Tread carefully. Don't mistake the free love on offer as a genuine symbol of affection. Even if the expressed desire is spontaneous, claims of action and interest cannot be relied upon. Gently put them to one side, or they will do you harm.

Heart's Desire

Talking of health, I know how much you care about the well-being of your heart, so take a look at this idea for a new cookery book.

Cooking for a Healthy Heart
*Naturally healthy food that is good for
your heart and tastes great*

What do you think? It seems like an excellent idea. Surely everyone would want a book of recipes that promises a healthy heart without compromising on taste. When you ask people whether they would want the book, you get three typically enthusiastic responses:

1. I'm useless at cooking healthy food for myself, so that would come in handy. It would spur me on. When's it coming out?

2. I love browsing through cookbooks. These recipes look delicious and they're good for you. What more could anyone want. You can never have too many cookbooks. When's it coming out?

3. I don't like cooking and healthy food is tasteless. But I know someone who would enjoy this. It's the perfect present. When's it coming out?

Hooray! They want my book. The question is, who's telling the truth? The newly inspired non-cookbook buyer, the cookbook enthusiast or the considerate gifter? None of them, of course. Give yourself a pat on the back. The first doesn't like cooking, so their promises are worthless. If the second was genuinely motivated, they would have bought one of the many similar books on Amazon already. And the third is a magpie, attracted to whatever shiny new present is dangled before their eyes.

When you ask about desire, even the most sceptical of respondents is likely to say, 'Yes, I am interested. I would seriously consider buying your book.' But their desire is an illusion. Unless, of course, you happen to be the nation's favourite fitness instructor with a million avid followers on Instagram and a weekly 'Cooking for a Healthy Heart' programme on the BBC. Then you've got a bestseller on your hands. But, like the supposed desire for your idea, that person may be hard to find.

Put Your Money Where Your Mouth Is

There's a game you can play to discover whether or not the desire for your idea is genuine. It's called the 'Put your money where your mouth is' game. The premise is simple: If people express desire for your idea, ask them for cash to contribute towards its development, there and then.

Let me give you an example of how the game works. After being presented with a range of fundraising ideas for a wildlife conversation charity, research participants tend to be pretty fired up about which concept would most encourage them to give to the cause. 'I can't bear to think of these wonderful creatures pushed to the edge of extinction,' they weep. 'I would happily donate £10 to pay for their protection, without hesitation.'

But if you put a summary of each of the fundraising options on the table in front of them, ask them to get out their wallet or purse and place some money on to the concept they care about the most, your game players will look at you like you're mad. And tellingly, nobody will move a muscle. People don't want to hand over their hard-earned cash. Poor old Harold the Hedgehog is going to have to fend for himself.

In the world of asking, talk is cheap. Without a stake in the game, expressions of giving, clicking, sharing or buying are worthless. Action does not just speak louder than words; action is different to words.

Words are illusions.

When we ask people what they think, intention is a wildly inaccurate measure of success. The further an idea is from the finished article, the more ridiculous claims of desire become. Should you ever encounter the alluring phrase 'Intention to purchase' on your travels, my advice is simple: Run! Run as fast as you can. And keep on running for as long as your healthy heart will hold out.

Finding a desirable solution

The illusion of desire is a tricky problem with a surprisingly obvious solution: Don't ask the question. Working out how desirable your idea may or may not be is an integral part of asking, but posing the question is pointless. The response isn't real. Tempting though it may be to ask, 'Do you want my idea?' the question or any of its many derivations is best avoided. Because once you've asked, it's incredibly difficult to resist the answer.

There is a reason why desire sits at the heart of the wheel. It's because the degree to which an idea is genuinely engaging is a function of its appeal, purpose, relevance, impact, clarity, credibility and personality combined. If you make the effort to understand the response to each of the wonders, you'll be able to work out the desirability of your idea without the need to ask.

It's not that we're trying to avoid the issue of desire. Far from it. We just want to deal with it properly. The whole point of asking for feedback is to maximise the potential of an idea, but rather than naively trusting the answers to be real, we're taking control of the question. Working out desire is our responsibility. The one, more than any other, we can neither abdicate nor delegate. It may be impossible to launch, create or do something of value without asking our intended audience for their opinion, but when it comes to deciding whether or not an idea is going to be desirable, and how to make it more so, we have to figure that out for ourselves.

Time for a Cocktail

It's been a long drive, but boy oh boy has it been worth it. We've arrived at the most picturesque of destinations: Success! No-one can say we haven't eaten well along the way. We've stopped off at McDonald's for a cheeky burger, enjoyed a tender cooked chicken breast and a generous bowl of salad at our local Harvester, and grabbed a frozen Lamb Tagine from Cook to pop in the oven when we get home. I don't know about you, I could do with a drink. And not just any old drink, but a fabulous strawberry mojito, made from seven wonderful ingredients:

- Appealing strawberries
- Purposeful white rum
- Relevant sugar syrup
- Impactful lime
- Clarity crushed ice
- Believable club soda
- Personality mint

Relaxing on the beach, as the sun sets on another hard day of listening and the over-sized moon begins to appear over the horizon, remember there is nothing to be gained from asking people if they want your idea. Desire is a cocktail you have to mix yourself. And if the people you are asking want one, they are going to have to pay for it themselves. Cheers.

13

The Illusion Index

There is one important question that remains unresolved: Are all the wonders of the world of asking distorted to the same extent or are some of the illusions more exaggerated than others?

The illusion index attempts to answer that question.

Measuring illusions is not an exact science. There are limits as to how precise you can be because, depending on the nature of your business and the idiosyncrasies of your idea, different illusions will dominate. For example, if you are researching initiatives designed to encourage people to take action to preserve nature, the illusion of relevance is likely to present the greatest challenge. The resonance of your idea will almost certainly be at odds with what people do. Alternatively, if you are trying to create something original and thought-provoking, then the illusion of appeal will work hardest to lead you astray. Your audience will be inclined to reject your idea in favour of the familiar and similar.

Nonetheless, some illusions do consistently pose a more significant level of threat than others. Derived from the findings of hundreds of research projects and the opinions of thousands of respondents, the illusion index provides a sound indicator of the intensity of the trouble that awaits.

Explaining the Index

The index uses a simple scale from one to ten, where a score of one signifies the response is a perfect mirror image of the real world, and a score of ten represents a total distortion of reality. The chart below provides an overview of the illusion index for each of the wonders.

The Illusion Index

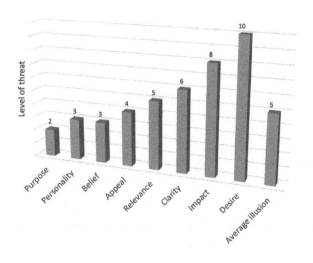

Let's have a look at the scores, in ascending order of the level of threat, and remind ourselves of what can be done to mitigate the effects.

Purpose
Illusion index: two

In theory, the illusion of purpose is the least scary of all the illusions. After all, it's not difficult to assess what an idea does or is supposed to do. But beware. If the purpose of your idea lacks authenticity and integrity, asking your intended audience what they think has the potential to make things far, far worse. Since those being asked can only respond to what you put in front of them, they have little choice but to collude in the fantasy you are trying to create. Without a keen sense of what you stand for, asking people what they think can end in disaster.

Illusion buster: Be true

Personality
Illusion index: three

The illusion of personality has two faces. The artificially attentive world of asking overstates the depth of an idea's personality and allows the superficial to thrive. In real life, detailed characteristics are harder to spot, relationships take longer to build and contrived personalities are liable to crack. The secret is to avoid getting carried away with the fanciful image reflecting back at you and concentrate instead on forging a meaningful relationship between your personality and your purpose, between who you are and what you stand for.

Illusion buster: Simplicity and sincerity

Belief

Illusion index: three

In the world of asking, people lose their ability to respond intuitively and emotionally. They think rather than feel. Consequently, they crave facts and further information. Don't be fooled. These requests for evidence are merely an expression of rejection and resistance in disguise. In the real world, your product is your proof, facts are dull and more information is the preserve of the predisposed. Put your faith in feelings. Create more relaxed environments for asking, encourage intuitive response and ignore the constant demands for proof.

Illusion buster: Feelings before facts

Appeal

Illusion index: four

Appeal is overstated, but not by as much as you might think. For sure, people tend to be gentler on ideas in the world of asking than they would be in the real world, but if you encourage them to give you their honest opinion, they can be as critical as they are kind – particularly online. The greater danger is caused by our obsession with appeal. We love our ideas to be liked. We need our ideas to be liked. We forget people prefer the familiar and similar. We put appeal on a pedestal and magnify its importance out of all proportion. As a result, the illusion of appeal is twice the strength it would otherwise be.

Illusion buster: Ask yourself why

Relevance

Illusion index: five

Just thinking about an idea makes it disproportionately relevant. People are naturally self-centred, so 'What's in it for me?' is the start-point for any response. Moreover, good intentions and an inclination to please only serve to further exaggerate the perceived relevance of an idea. Ultimately, the extent of the threat posed by the illusion of relevance depends almost entirely on your ability to reframe the response in the context of your consumers' lives.

Illusion buster: Depend on do

Clarity

Illusion index: six

The act of asking has a nasty habit of making things seem much clearer than they really are. The effort people put into understanding an idea bears no relation to how they would behave in the real world. The way we set up and explain our ideas often makes the problem worse. However, if we keep our wits about us, watch out for signs of the penny dropping, avoid the trap of selling and resolve any issues of clarity before we move on, then the cloudy skies should clear.

Illusion buster: Let your idea do the talking

Impact

Illusion index: eight

The undistracted, uncompetitive version of impact we experience in the world of asking is a far cry from the ongoing battle to remain top of mind in the real world. To combat the illusion of impact, we must look beyond stand out and distinctiveness in the here and now, and focus our energies on asking the intelligent questions that will enable us to accurately assess the barriers, triggers, opportunities and threats awaiting our idea in the world to come.

Illusion buster: Prepare for battle

Desire

Illusion index: ten

The illusion of desire is the grandest and greatest illusion of them all – a potent cocktail of all the other distortions, exaggerations and biases combined. There are no mitigating factors or extenuating circumstances. When we ask people what they think, we cannot rely on expressions of desire, good or bad, prompted or spontaneous. Evaluating desirability is our responsibility and ours alone.

Illusion buster: Work it out

Mean Streets

If you take the mean score of all the illusions combined, the average distortion is five. Therefore, the response when you ask people what they think is, on average, five times greater than it would be in the real world. That is huge. The size of the illusion should serve as a sobering reminder of how overblown response can be. By recognising the scale of the twisted truth, you will be able to retain a tighter grip on what people genuinely think of your ideas and be better placed to work out what to do as a result. If you remain reluctant to acknowledge the size of the gap between asked-for answers and real-world responses, then you probably stand a one in five chance of making good decisions based on what other people think. Which would explain why eighty per cent of businesses fail.

Nearly There

In theory, asking people for their opinions should be a precursor of success. Putting the needs of your customers first should guarantee the development of appealing, purposeful, relevant, impactful, clear, believable, personable and desirable ideas. In practice, the rocky road of response is fraught with danger.

Thankfully, the Wonder Wheel is on hand to help you navigate the mean streets of asking. Take hold of the wheel.

Use it to keep yourself out of trouble. From what I've seen over the years, there is no right or wrong way to drive. Your inclination may be to wind your way slowly through the scenic pathways of consumer insight, enthusiastically exploring every element of response in all its glory. Or perhaps you prefer to keep the asking short and sweet, only briefly stopping off to admire the wonders of the world of asking before speeding on your way to your intended destination. Either way, the only thing that truly matters is that you're the one driving the car.

END OF PART ONE

A Quick Break

If you take a look under the umpire's chair at the Wimbledon Tennis Championships, you'll see bottles of Robinsons Lemon Barley Water. It's been that way since the 1930s when Eric Smedley Hodgson came up with the recipe to refresh and hydrate the players. The connection between Robinson's Barley Water and Wimbledon is the second-longest partnership in the history of sport. The first is Slazenger, also from Wimbledon.

Imagine yourself as a ball girl or ball boy gracing Wimbledon's centre court. Serena Williams sits calmly in her chair, readying herself for the deciding set of a tense women's final. She calls you over and asks for a cold glass of delicious, rehydrating Robinsons Lemon Barley Water. You run to the umpire's chair, grab the bottle, pour a glass of squash and rush back to Serena. But in your excitement, you forget to dilute the squash. You've just poured the greatest female tennis player of all time a glass of undiluted concentrate. She spits it out. The crowd gasps in horror. The umpire asks for you to be removed from the court. You sit alone in the changing room, head in hands, sobbing quietly to yourself. 'How could I do such a thing? Who wouldn't dilute a concentrate? How could I have been so stupid?'

When you ask people what they think, they focus. Their response is inevitably and unavoidably a concentrated version of the real thing. It makes as much sense to swallow undiluted opinions as it does to drink a glass of undiluted squash. Next time you consider taking feedback at face value, imagine yourself gagging on a glass of undiluted Robinsons Lemon Barley Water. Don't do it. It is a foolish thing to do.

The crucial question is not, 'Should I add water?' but rather, 'How much water should I add? How much do I need to dilute the response?' The answer is five. Five-parts water to one-part response. That is the solution to all your 'What do you think' woes. And, weirdly enough, it also makes a very nice glass of squash.

'A long time ago, when the earth was very young, it was one huge garden covered in tall palm trees and perfumed jasmine, and the songs of nightingales flooded the landscape with their gentle melodies. At this time, all men were loyal, trustworthy and honest. In fact, the word 'lie' did not even exist.

But one day, someone told a lie. It was a very small lie and of no importance, but it was the end of man's childhood and the age of innocence.

So God summoned all the men on the earth together and said to them, 'Each time one of you lies, I shall throw a grain of sand onto the earth.'

The men looked at each other, shrugged their shoulders and said to themselves, 'A grain of sand? What difference will that make? You can hardly see a grain of sand.'

And so lie after lie, little by little, the Sahara gradually came into existence, as God threw grains of sand onto the earth from the heavens above. But here and there the odd oasis can still be seen. These are the traces of the original garden, because not all men lie.'

The Birth of the Sahara
by Ahmed Temiicha: Marrakesh storyteller [10]

Part Two

TRUTH

14

Marrakesh Syndrome

Meaning of *Marrakesh syndrome*

Marrakesh syndrome:

a group of consistently occurring symptoms
that cause research responses to become
unreliable. The condition can result in confusion,
delusion and poor decision-making

I've been to Marrakesh twice. The first time was for
business and I stayed in a purpose-built, conference
style, pseudo-Moroccan hotel, situated about half an
hour from the centre of the old city. Aside from a brief
opportunity to run into the souk to buy a fez and take a
selfie with a snake charmer, I didn't feel like I'd captured
the full Marrakesh experience. So, my wife and I decided to
go for a long weekend.

With four young kids at home, a weekend away without the children was a major event. We couldn't wait. Everything we heard about Marrakesh only added to our excitement. Friends, family and colleagues spoke as one. 'Marrakesh is fabulous!' they enthused. 'You'll love it.'

But we didn't love it. We thought Marrakesh was miserable. It was cold, rainy, dirty and a constant hassle. It was the antithesis of all we had hoped for. I'm sure Marrakesh holds delights for many, but we didn't like it.

On our return, we were greeted with a familiar question.

'What did you think of Marrakesh?' everyone asked expectantly. 'Isn't it amazing?'

'It was lovely,' we replied. 'We had a great time.'

Why did we do that? Why didn't we reveal our true feelings? Why did we hold back? For all kinds of reasons: Firstly, we didn't want to let down those hopeful of a positive response. Family and friends had put so much energy into looking after the kids, it would have been awful to suggest their efforts had been wasted. Secondly, we reinterpreted the experience for our own benefit. We wanted to remember our precious time off with affection. Thirdly, we felt a bit stupid. If you don't like something everyone else loves, it's tempting to blame yourself. Marrakesh is fine. The idea is fine. The problem is me. And finally, we couldn't be bothered to tell the truth. Why set ourselves up as adversaries of Marrakesh? To challenge perceived wisdom is hard work. It's easier to go with the flow and conform. So, we kept schtum. Even now, it makes me nervous to tell you how I really feel about Marrakesh. I know you're judging me. I can feel it.

The saving grace was the riad we stayed in – a tranquil oasis nestled amidst the madness that is Marrakesh. It was lovely. So much so, I wrote a glowing review and posted it on TripAdvisor. What the review doesn't say is that the riad was owned by a friend's aunt, which was one of the reasons we went to Marrakesh in the first place. I felt compelled to write an overly enthusiastic review. It would have been churlish not to. Anyway, my opinion is just one amongst many, so what difference does it make if my comments are only half true?

A Chance Encounter

Soon after our return, I was on the bus minding my own business when the guy alongside me said, 'I think I was sitting at the table next to you in a café in Marrakesh last week.' What are the chances!

Naturally he asked, 'What did you think of Marrakesh?'

Caught off guard, I shrugged and mumbled, 'I thought it was a bit of a dump.'

'So did I,' he exclaimed.

We were so excited we hugged each other. Two strangers cuddling on the bus! The relief was enormous. In the company of a kindred spirit, we could both finally be honest. It just goes to show – the truth is out there. If you ask the right person in the right place at the right time, you might be lucky enough to get a glimpse of what they really think.

A couple of months later, we had dinner with good friends Brian and Dido. They'd recently returned from a few days in Marrakesh and they loved it. Brian was there for work, so they were on expenses. They had a great time. In fact, over the years I've met many people who stead-fastly maintain they adored Marrakesh. And not all of them stayed at the Four Seasons. So, in due deference to all you Marrakesh enthusiasts, I happily acknowledge that ours may not be a universal truth. That is the trouble with asking people what they think – not everyone has the same opinion. Asking is easy. The hard part is working out who to listen to and who to ignore.

The Passage of Time

A few months ago, I read an article in the paper by a journalist who'd spent a week in Marrakesh. Poor mad fool. For the first few days his experience was similar to ours. Then things changed. Street hawkers and vendors ceased trying to sell him ancient artefacts. Guides to the souk started to leave him alone. The pace of the place slowed around him. He gave off a different vibe and the city responded. Mad though it seems, Marrakesh changed.

Time spent with someone or something changes it and them and you. Even inanimate objects bend and flex and change as your relationship with them develops. Some relationships change for the better, some for the worse, but change they do.

An entire city can change around you.

The person who has been in Marrakesh for three days is not the same as the person who has been there for seven. And indeed, over time, my views have mellowed. I have wonderful memories of Marrakesh. What may have once been my truth is now no longer the case. Even actual experiences change on reflection. If you asked me what I think of Marrakesh today, I wouldn't know what to say.

15

Making Demands

'I believe that Marrakesh ought to be earned as a
destination. The journey is the preparation for
the experience. Reaching it too fast derides it,
makes it a little less easy to understand.'

In Arabian Nights by Tahir Shah[11]

P art One of this book is about understanding response.
Part Two is about finding truth. Up to this point,
we've worked on the basis that what people say is
an honest reflection of what they think. It is the artificial
focus on the idea that causes their response to become
unreliable. Part Two starts from a rather different place. It
assumes people are not telling us the truth.

The Research Effect

Even if you haven't given a moment's thought to the concept of 'the research effect', you could probably make a pretty good stab at what it is. It refers to the well-documented principle that involving people in a research task influences how they think and behave. In the world of asking, these influences are known as, among other things, demand characteristics. Demand characteristics describe the ways in which people alter their thoughts and behaviours when you ask something of them, i.e. make a demand. When you ask people for their opinions, there isn't one single effect; there's a whole stack of them. The only way to get a true sense of the breadth and depth of these characteristics is to experience them yourself.

The 'I've got an idea' Game

To help you on your way, I've created the 'I've got an idea' game. You can play it at home with your kids, in the office with colleagues, or relaxing in a rooftop café overlooking Jemaa el-Fnaa, the beating heart of old Marrakesh. It's a game for two or more players and the rules are as follows: Each person playing comes up with an idea. You take it in turns to explain your idea to the other players and they have to say what they think. There are no restrictions on the idea. It doesn't have to be big or brilliant, clever or funny, new or different. It just has to be your idea. You can go in any order, but everyone must have a turn. Yes, if you want, the youngest can start. Here are some examples of ideas. They're not mine, so don't worry about offending me. All I want is your honest opinion.[12]

Idea One: Jack's idea

Men rarely miss calls because their mobile phone vibrates in their trouser pocket. Women often miss calls, especially in noisy social situations, because they keep their phone in their handbag. My idea is to come up with a line of jewellery in partnership with Tiffany, which would vibrate when your phone rings.

Idea Two: Nicki's idea

There are times when your date doesn't turn up, or it wasn't a great experience, or the things people have said about themselves turn out not to be true. My idea is to have a dating app with a section where you can leave feedback after a date. It could be a private function reserved for friends rather than everyone. Rate dates for mates.

Idea Three: Tom's idea

I have four sisters and they like to bake. My idea is to spice it up by having tiny helium balloons you attach to the cake to create a very colourful affair. The miniature balloons come in a pack with attractive ribbons and a small can of helium. Tiny decorative balloons.

Idea Four: Jane's idea

Jon's, I mean Jane's idea, is a classic board game. The aim of the game is to be the first to find your way around the souk in Marrakesh, collecting souvenirs as you go – slippers, spices, antiques, fezzes, a selfie with a snake charmer – you get the idea. Guess what it's called? That's right. Marrakesh! What a brilliant idea.

It's incredibly easy to form opinions about something we know little if anything about. Yet even more remarkable is the extraordinary texture and complexity of thought that underpins our instinctive reactions.

It's nice to be asked what we think. It's a good feeling. The person asking is sharing with us something of their own making. They are putting their trust in us. We feel valued. We want to be kind to the owner of the idea in return, so we couch our true feelings in a veneer of positivity. We say, 'I like the concept of wearing a bracelet that tells me if my phone is ringing.' We avoid saying, 'That idea already exists, you fool. It's called the Apple Watch. And why on earth would Tiffany do something so crass?' We are wary of saying how we truly feel for fear of causing upset. We censor our responses.

But it's a careful balance. We know, in our heart of hearts, the idea is unworkable, so we don't want to egg the idea owner on. We try to judge how much the person doing the asking values our opinion before deciding how to respond. We feel the weight of their expectations. We become cautious. We don't want to be wrong. After all, we're not experts on vibrating jewellery and mini cake decorations. We ask ourselves, 'Is my opinion valid?'

We remain constantly aware of our fellow players. We take our cue from the tone of their response. We admire the clarity of their point of view. We too, want to be seen to have a good opinion. We might even compete to sound clever. We build on their comments.

And what happens if we can't think of anything worthwhile to say? Does that mean we don't care about the person doing the asking? Surely, it's better to make something up than it is to say nothing at all.

Don't forget, it's our turn next. While listening to the ideas of others, we've got to think about our own idea. We only have half a mind on what we are being asked about. Mostly, we're thinking about ourselves. 'Twas ever thus, game or no game.

Just a Game

Next time you ask someone, 'What do you think?' remember buzzing bracelets and tiny helium balloons. For the idea owner, asking is a serious business, but for the person being asked, it's just a game – a game without cost or consequence. Giving your opinions is pure playtime. In fact, if you are lucky, you can even be paid to play. There may only be a couple of formal instructions: 'Look at this idea, listen to this idea, tell me what you think.' But beyond these explicit demands, there lies a raft of implicit expectations. These are the unwritten rules of the game.

When someone asks us what we think, we are influenced by a myriad of cultural biases and psychological effects. In behavioural science speak, we acquiesce, we social norm, we conform and we play the role of the good participant. Being asked, 'What do you think of my idea?' is not really an ask, it's a demand. A demand to be nice, to value, to be considerate, to care. In an instant, we process what is expected and required of us. We don't try to behave differently, we just do. We are changed by the asking.

Naming each of the strands of our flawed response implies you can pull them apart. You can't. They're all mixed up. You can no more separate the individual biases that influence, determine and make up our responses than you can distinguish the ingredients of a lamb and apricot tagine, blended and baked for hour upon hour. You can admire the tender pieces of lamb, perhaps even exclaim excitedly when you spy the odd apricot, but the rich flavours and delicate spices, the magical infusion of cardamom, cumin, ginger, honey and cinnamon, remain tantalisingly out of sight.

Getting to grips with the illusion of interest is not enough. What is the point in putting all that effort into decoding the wonders of the world of asking if we can't even trust what people say? We need to find a way of getting closer to the truth. We have to come up with a sufficiently simple set of instructions for the game of asking that will enable our respondents to say how they truly feel. We need to work out how to make good decisions off the back of other people's opinions when we can't trust the person, as well as their words. Most of all, we need to know what is causing that annoying buzzing noise. Oh, I know what it is. It's my wife's mobile phone ringing in her handbag. Someone really needs to invent a way of sorting that out.

16

Hidden Forces

In 2006, Kathleen D Vohs, a professor at the University of Minnesota's Carlson School of Management, published a paper called *The Psychological Consequences of Money*. The paper described what happened when subjects were primed with images of cash. For example, when given a choice of partners, people who had stared at a money-related screensaver ended up seating themselves farther away from a conversational partner.[13]

A series of experiments published in the *Journal of Experimental Social Psychology* also found that people primed with financial images were more likely to conceal their inner feelings. When asked to perform various tasks – such as writing negative reviews on Amazon – those subjects shown pictures of money were more reluctant to express their emotions than those who viewed images such as seashells, furniture or leaves.[14]

There are hundreds of published studies on priming, all of which point to the same conclusion: when we ask people what they think, their response is subconsciously primed by influences entirely out of their control. Something as simple as seeing a picture of money makes a difference to who they want to sit next to, what they value, what they say and their ability to express their feelings.

Being involved in a financial negotiation, spending money, seeing a £5 note on the table, picking up a 10p coin from the floor, playing Monopoly, checking the value of your pension, being sent a text with your bank balance, being given £50 before the start of a focus group, having the incentive withheld until after the group has finished, rewarding people for answering a questionnaire – it's all going to have an effect. We pay people to tell us how they feel about our ideas, yet the very act of giving them money inhibits their ability to express their feelings.

Trouble is, everything will have an effect. The weather, your day at work, hormones, how tired you are, cake, the crisps on the table, dieting, stress, *Game of Thrones*, the long ride home, thinking about your holiday, the state of your hair, shoes, shopping, needing a cigarette, needing a drink, Valium, *Breaking Bad*, how much charge you have left on your phone, your mum, your boss, your kids, Facebook, *Friends*, falling out, making up... everything! It's prime-time anarchy.

There's nothing we can do about the endless set of factors that subconsciously influence response. There's no such thing as a neutral environment for asking. Unprimed responses do not exist. Like the finest golfers in the world, we can practise playing in the wind, we can wait for the moment when the wind drops, we can use all our experience to work with the wind rather than against it, but we can't change the wind.

Priming is like the wind. It blows response off course and there is nothing we can do about it.

Sexual Healing

What do you think of this ten-second ad for Rightmove? [15]

We open on a baby's mobile with the planets revolving around the sun above a baby's cot. As the planets move, they momentarily form a straight line.

A female voiceover says: 'Going round, it was as if the house had been waiting just for us, like the planets had aligned.'

Cut to end frame. 'Rightmove. Find your happy.'

What are your thoughts? Respondents in research groups liked the idea. But not Sangeeta. She hated the ad with a passion. The first thing she said was, 'Why are there no men in the advert? Having a woman at home looking after the children is a stereotypical view of society. The role of women is under relentless attack from unconscious gender bias, and this ad typifies that pernicious and pervasive hidden threat. I hate it!'

Sangeeta may well be right. The ad may be a telling symbol of unconscious gender bias, or it could just be an ad featuring a baby's mobile and a female voice. Either way, it's not important. Well, it is, but it isn't.

At the beginning of the discussion, I asked participants to introduce themselves. Sangeeta explained she'd just come back from a year in India as a mature student researching gender studies and the role of women in Indian society. Sangeeta's experience defined the lens through which she saw the ad. There was a straight-line connection between her 'personal agenda' and her 'response agenda'. I knew it, everyone in the room knew it and I suspect Sangeeta knew it too. You couldn't really miss it.

Whenever we ask people for feedback, they will always have a personal agenda that will affect their response. But unlike the obvious impact on the thoughts and feelings of Sangeeta, most of the time, we won't know it.

Here's another one of those subversive ten-second ads for Rightmove.

We open on a plastic toy hula girl wobbling on the dashboard of a car. When the voices of the happy movers being interviewed in their car become more animated, the hula girl's wobbles increase.

*Off camera, two young women chat. 'You've got to
be on it when you are renting. As soon as we saw
this place, we were straight round, weren't we?
I could do a little dance!'*

Cut to end frame. 'Rightmove. Find your happy.'

Unsurprisingly, respondents weren't that fussed either way.
But not Andy. He loved it.

'That's going to grab everyone's attention,' he enthused,
'because the hula girl is so sexual. It's designed to turn
you on. It certainly got me.'

'Then again,' Andy continued unabashed, 'I had sex
with my girlfriend just before I came to the group and
I've got sex on the brain.'

Two people, two very different drivers of response. One
had spent the previous year of her life researching gender
inequality, the other had recently explored the issue of
gender difference in an altogether more hands-on way.
Both experiences were equal in the effect they had on
response. Both respondents wore their heart on their sleeve;
what was on their minds came out of their mouths.

That's not normal. The connection between influence
and response is rarely so transparent and openly expressed.
Usually, when we ask someone what they think, what we
don't know will almost certainly be greater than what we
do. What we can't know will almost always outweigh what
we can. In most cases, we have no idea. We are fumbling
around in the dark.

Biting Your Tongue

I was an innocent bystander at a meeting between my client and their ad agency. The marketing director and marketing manager were being presented with creative ideas for a new campaign. Once approved, the work would then be put into research. The reaction to the concepts was resoundingly positive. With great enthusiasm, the marketing director told the agency how delighted she was. Apparently, two of the ideas were so good it was going to be difficult to choose between them. She had a tingling feeling in her tummy. That was a good sign.

On leaving the agency, I jumped in a cab with my clients. As soon as the car door was closed, they began to express their intense disappointment at the quality of the concepts they'd been shown. The work wasn't up to scratch. The ideas bore no relation to what they'd been expecting. None of the ideas even met the brief. They were angry and frustrated. That was a bad sign.

Based on their response in the meeting, I was totally convinced everything was hunky-dory. Neither the agency nor I could possibly have known they were displeased. Nothing about their demeanour indicated their dissatisfaction. It was as though I had entered a parallel universe where expressed thoughts were diametrically opposed to true feelings. So, I asked the marketing director, 'If you weren't happy, why didn't you say? Why didn't you tell them what you really thought?'

'I couldn't say how I felt in the meeting,' my client explained, 'I had to bite my tongue.'

Why did she do that? It sounds so painful. Why do we do that? What is the point? I'm glad you asked. There are many reasons why we bite our tongues.

1. **Trust:** It is easier to reveal our true feelings to trusted friends and colleagues than it is to expose our instinctive thoughts to a group of people who are not part of our inner circle.

2. **Double-checking:** We hold fire because we want to verify our reactions. Maybe we are missing something. Sensibly, we don't want to mouth-off until we have had a private opportunity to collect our thoughts.

3. **Learning from others:** It can be helpful to consider other people's views before finalising how we feel. Particularly those we most respect. For example, the marketing director knew the opinions of clever colleagues back at the office would only enhance her ability to judge.

4. **Consequences:** Honesty can have serious repercussions. In this instance, it was my client who had briefed the agency. If the work wasn't up to scratch, it was her fault. Ultimately, she was responsible. The sub-standard ideas would reflect badly on her. She was going to have to think carefully about how best to manage her response.

5. **Good relations:** People don't like to be criticised.
   Had the marketing director expressed her true
   feelings, it could have undermined the working
   relationship she had been trying so hard to build.
   Unrestrained responses are rarely compatible with
   healthy relationships. Holding back helps us get along.

6. **Patience:** Finally, why not wait? Invariably,
   reservations and concerns will come out in the wash.
   There is little to be gained from knee-jerk reactions.
   Problems can be dealt with tomorrow. There's no
   rush to be honest.

All things considered, withholding is often a very wise
move. Think of the times you have consciously refrained
from revealing the full force of your unfiltered opinions.
Your actions were not devious, underhand, cowardly or
deliberately dishonest. At worst, you were being wary. At
best, you were playing smart. Your motivations may well
have been positive, considered and constructive. Sometimes, saying what you think is simply not worth the trouble.
For the marketing director, having a sore tongue was not
the biggest deal. The unsuspecting agency was under a
false impression for a couple of days, but that was all. The
end result would be pretty much the same – they would
have to amend the work anyway – it was only the timing
of the news that had changed.

Yet the upshot of tongue-biting is not always so benign.
If people suppress their true feelings, we seldom get the

chance to find out what they really believed. More often than not, we are stuck with the deception. Whatever the consequences, serious or otherwise, concealing the truth is a choice. People know they're not giving the whole game away. In the world of asking, respondents are masters of their own hidden opinions as much as they are the unwitting victims of forces over which they have no control.

The Woman with the Blue Hair

I was feeling overwhelmed by the unsettling implications of uncertain response, so I decided to attend a conference on British manufacturing. Sitting a few seats along from me was a woman with bright blue hair. At the end of one of the talks, the chair of the session asked the audience if they had any questions, and the hand belonging to the woman with the bright blue hair shot up.

The chairperson pointed to her and said, 'The woman with the blue hair.'

So we could all hear the question, an eager young helper rushed over with a microphone, but instead of speaking, the woman with the blue hair held tightly on to the mic, laughing. It was one of the oddest things I have ever seen. She continued giggling for what seemed like an age. Eventually, she composed herself.

'I'm sorry,' she said, 'It's just nobody has ever called me that before.'

And I thought, 'What! What do you mean, nobody has ever called you that before? You've got bright blue hair!' How is that possible? Surely, someone at some point must have said to her, 'Wow! You really do have extraordinarily blue hair.' One thing is certain. They may not have said it, but they definitely thought it.

It just goes to show, often even the most obvious of thoughts stay firmly fixed in our heads. Our tongues as silent as they are sore.

The Meaning of Marrakesh Syndrome

The world of asking is a richly textured land of lies, half-truths, social niceties, self-censored responses, weighed-up opinions and introspection. It is a place where people play games. In doing so, they follow a well-established set of instructions and demands that are both explicit and implicit. And that's just for starters. Beyond the boundaries of our knowledge, understanding and control, there lies a further infinite realm of primed responses, hidden subtext and holding back.

This astonishing collection of research effects come together to forge a second defining principle of asking that is every bit as influential as the illusion of interest:

**In the land of asking,
there is no such thing as *the* truth.**

When we ask people what they think, the expectation of a concrete answer, a definitive number or even a clear understanding, misses the point and causes all the trouble. We cannot be sure of the answer. To believe otherwise lacks humanity and humility. When we make decisions founded on what people think, we do so in the full and certain knowledge that the asking is flawed. Our aim should be to work towards truth rather than to profess we have found truth. The asking guides us towards *an* answer, but it is not *the* answer.

'Music begins where the
possibilities of language end'

Sibelius

17

Compose Yourself

Our journey on the road to enlightenment begins with a deeper understanding of our fellow travelling companions. The following map is designed to help:

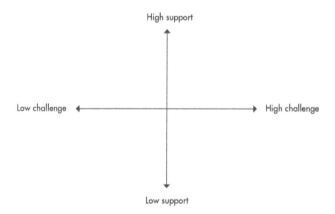

The world of asking spins upon two axes:

Axis One is a supporter axis – how inclined your respondents are to be on your side.

Axis Two is a challenger axis – how keen they are to tell you what you've got wrong.

Within these axes sit four dominant types of respondent: Supporters, Developers, Critics and the Disinterested.

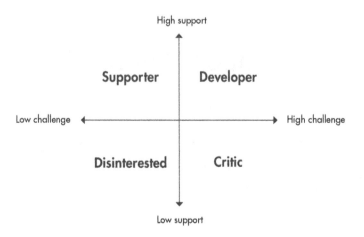

By way of a brief introduction:

- The Supporter thinks your idea is great
- The Developer tells you how to do it better
- The Critic points out what is wrong with your idea
- The Disinterested can't be bothered with it

Whatever you're asking about, whether it be a new low-calorie ice cream, behavioural interventions designed to reduce knife crime, or your new shoes, you'll always find the Supporter, Developer, Critic and Disinterested.

Take a look at the fundraising concept on the following page. Let's assume for a moment, all those being asked for

their opinion support cancer charities and enjoy cake. In other words, they should be positively predisposed to the idea. Even so, there are four types of response:

- Supporter: "I love the idea. It's a tasty twist on the usual cake sale. Bring on the baking.'

- Developer: 'It's a fun idea, but you need to include a date for the event and a link to fruity cake recipes.'

- Critic: 'Why are you complicating a simple concept? Fruit cake is a hassle to make. It's a silly idea.'

- Disinterested: 'I don't even know what 'Bake Fruity' means and I'm not inclined to find out.'

Depending on our mood, the person doing the asking, the question being asked and the idea itself, we can be any or all of these responder archetypes. Each of us has the capacity to support, develop, critique and be disinterested.

The question is, which one do you listen to?

The answer is all of them.

All four are necessary to make the world go round. Each has a distinct part to play in our quest for truth. Even the scantest recognition of the differences between these four types of respondent will help you ask better questions, listen more attentively to the answers and make improved judgements as a result.

The Supporter

The supporter will show you what is good about your idea. They focus on its strengths.

Typically, supporters will say:

That's brilliant.
That is the best idea I have ever heard.
You are so clever. How did you think of that?
Well done you!

When we have an idea, we seek out supporters to ask them what they think. When confronted with a range of opinions, we put a premium on the response of the supporter. But it's easy to forget they would have loved almost anything we showed them. Their desire to support overrides any genuine concerns they may have and divorces their response from their real-world beliefs and behaviours. Other names for supporters include lily gilders, turd polishers and Mum.

The Developer

A developer starts from the point of view of 'like', then focuses on what you could do better. Developers want to build on your idea. They emphasise its potential and help you explore its boundaries and possibilities. The developer is constructive. They can even be inspirational. They keep us on our toes. There is always room for improvement.

Developers are prone to say:

It's a good idea. But why don't you do it like this?
I know how you could improve it.
I've got a better idea for you.

Unfortunately, despite their desire to help, developers often use being asked as an opportunity to demonstrate their own cleverness and creativity. In doing so, they state the bleeding obvious and regurgitate impractical ideas that have long since been dismissed. Call them builders, iterators or developers; their role is to help improve your ideas – up to a point.

The Critic

Being a critic is fun. As Benjamin Disraeli said, 'It's easier to be critical than to be correct.' It's a sentiment that most of us can relate to. When it comes to new ideas, we are natural critics – quick to find fault, hard to impress, wary of new concepts and sceptical about claims made by brands, companies and governments alike.

The sorts of things critics say are:

I think that's shite.
I don't think I'd use it.
I'm not sure I believe you.

The critic may be harsh or they may be gentle. Either way, we can learn from them. In the words of another Benjamin, Franklin this time, 'Critics are our friends, they show us our faults.' The role of the critic is to point out failings, question relevance and highlight the strengths of the competition. The critic keeps the supporter in check.

The Disinterested

The disinterested should be engaged, but they are not. That may be because your idea is not sufficiently interesting to warrant much of an opinion or their minds may simply be elsewhere. Whatever the reason, they opt out. Their response is reluctant and platitudinous.

The disinterested are likely to say:

Have you seen this funny cat video?
I agree with what she said.
That's nice, dear.

The disinterested are a vital reminder that nobody is really interested in our ideas. When it comes to the real world, we are going to have to work hard to engage. In daily life, most people are disinterested the majority of the time. They've got better things to do. Without the disinterested we are suckers for the illusion of interest.

The Composer

Right in the middle of the map, at the centre of the world, sits the composer – part supporter, part developer, part critic and part disinterested.

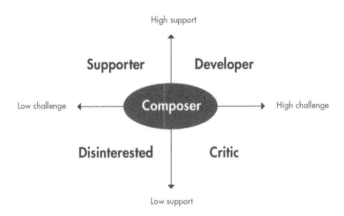

Composers can be encouraging and supportive, yet they also provide candid and honest feedback that may be uncomfortable or difficult to hear. Composers speak truthfully, but constructively, about weaknesses and problems. Like developers, composers remain open to possibility and continuously seek opportunities to improve. They are able to spot quick fixes and suggest practical solutions to more substantial problems. Composers are constantly aware of the ever-present impact and influence of the illusion of interest. A composer balances support, criticism, development and disinterest.

The composer is of course, you.

Truth and Composition

When you ask people what they think, they play games. Their thoughts and feelings are primed in a way that is beyond their knowledge and your control. A hidden subtext defines their response and for reasons known only to themselves, they withhold their true feelings.

In the world of asking, the truth is not given, it is composed. And you are the composer. Getting people to make a noise is easy, it's turning the noise into something meaningful that counts.

To make good decisions based on people's opinions, you must first gather together a collection of supporters, developers, critics and the disinterested. Then you can begin to compose. Think of yourself as the creator of a wonderful choral symphony. Yet unlike the soprano, alto, tenor and bass to be found in a traditional choir, the four voices in your choir of composition are not defined by age or gender. Whoever, whenever and wherever you choose to ask, you will always come across the enthusiastic cries of the supporter, the shrill comments of the critic, the assertive opinions of the developer and the rumbling discontent of the disinterested. All you need do is ask and the four voices of response will reveal themselves to you. Some of the members of your choir will lead, others will follow, but the beauty and the balance of the piece, the final composition, is down to you.

A Quick Review

Let me show you how the concept of composition plays out in our everyday lives.

If you're anything like me, you use customer reviews to help you make decisions about where to eat, which riad to book, what movies to watch, which headphones to buy, and who to call when your toilet is blocked. With a healthy dose of scepticism built-in, we are inclined to believe that the reviews on which we rely are genuinely written by people who have experienced the place, product or service in which we are interested.

Even so, we approach these opinions with caution and always, always use our critical faculties to work out their worth. We gather together a selection of reviews. We seek out good reviews, bad reviews and balanced reviews. We read between the lines, infer and interpret. We even try to get a sense from the style and tone of the review as to whether the reviewer is someone we can relate to and trust.

Using a set of well-honed and finely tuned skills, we carefully assess the credibility and value of a cross-section of reviews before deciding what to do next. Then, we compose. It is as natural for us to consider what the comments mean and then create our own composite review based on a spectrum of opinions as it is to consult the reviews in the first place. The bigger the investment, whether it be financial or emotional, the more effort we make to interpret and compose.

You know what's coming. Given our determination to create a composite review before deciding where we should go for dinner, it might be a good plan to spend a bit of time composing a meaningful truth, derived from a broad range of responses, before we make the decisions that will affect the future of our business.

The path to asking enlightenment is found through interpretation and composition. Our capacity to make wise decisions based on what other people think is defined by our ability to interpret response and compose truth. The Wonder Wheel is designed to help with the task of interpretation. The rest of this book is dedicated to the practice and development of our skills of composition.

18

The ACID Test

'If the soul is impartial in receiving information, it devotes to that information the share of critical investigation the information deserves, and its truth or untruth thus becomes clear. However, if the soul is infected with partisanship for a particular opinion or sect, it accepts without a moment's hesitation the information that is agreeable to it. Prejudice and partisanship obscure the critical faculty and preclude critical investigation. The result is that falsehoods are accepted and transmitted.'

Ibn Khaldun, 14th-Century North African philosopher. [16]

When we ask people what they think, our ability to compose is determined by the response we seek. That is not a new or radical thought. In fact, it's been around for 600 years. Our motivations for asking define our boundaries for listening. They determine who we ask, how we ask, what we ask and what we do.

What Is Your Real Reason for Asking?

Do you seek enlightenment?
Do you need help deciding what to do?
Do you lack confidence in your idea?
Are you looking to prove a point?
Are you justifying your choices?
Do you crave a clear outcome?
Do you need to be told how clever you are?
Are you covering your metaphorical arse?

Unless you acknowledge your own truth, you will never be able to truly understand response. Often, the actions we take prove incorrect, not because of the unreliability of other people's opinions, but because the real reason for asking remains unacknowledged.

The good news is that you don't have to pay for expensive therapy to peel away the layers and reveal your deep-seated inner motivations for asking people what they think. Ultimately, the universal need to ask comes down to your infant relationship with your mother. Not really. It's a bit more straightforward than that. All in all, there are only four reasons why we ask people what they think:

1. **Affirmation**
2. **Confidence**
3. **Insight**
4. **Decision**

By understanding our reasons for asking, we can begin to recognise the effect they have on us and what we choose to do as a result. That is the ACID test.

To illustrate the importance of the ACID test, I'm going to enlist the help of a new board game called Marrakesh. The game is at an early stage of development, and Jane, its creator, is keen to test the concept with her target audience. The brief remains the same – have a look at my idea and tell me what you think – is it likeable, purposeful, relevant, impactful, easy to understand, credible and fun? But depending on Jane's motives for asking, her approach to composition changes.

Looking for Affirmation

Jane believes her game to be good and wants to know you feel the same way. She's determined to demonstrate the potential of her idea to her boss and secure the necessary investment to enable her to progress to the next stage of development. Jane is on the hunt for validation and ammunition. As you would expect, she focuses on what people like about the idea, who it appeals to most and how much they are prepared to pay for it. Her field of vision is narrow. Those looking for affirmation gather round their supporters, intent on celebrating the responses that positively affirm their point of view.

Jane's composition is lopsided.

Looking for Confidence

Jane believes Marrakesh is probably a good idea, but she has reservations. She is worried the game lasts too long, the instructions are too complicated and the pieces too fiddly. Because Jane lacks confidence in her idea, what the intended audience don't like about Marrakesh is as important to her as what they do.

Those in need of confidence welcome enthusiasm and energy around their idea. Yet they also remain sensitive to negative comments, on high alert for the signs and signals that reflect any concerns they may have. Given that the most common driver for asking people what they think stems from a lack of confidence, it is hardly surprising we so often find ourselves swayed and buffeted by the inconsistencies of response.

Jane is battling with the wind.

Her composition is a mess.

Looking for Insight

Jane has no agenda. She simply wants to know more about her intended audience and their game-playing habits. She's keen to understand how they experience and interact with Marrakesh, without prejudice.

Jane is equally open to the comments of the supporter, the developer and the critic. She'll take on board a range of different perspectives and then apply all she has learnt to the development of her idea. However, caught up in her desire to listen and learn, Jane is prone to believe what people say. She is susceptible to the illusions that characterise response and likely to listen hardest to the most engaged. It is tempting to dismiss the disinterested when hungry for knowledge.

Jane is in a good place to compose.

But trouble still lurks at every corner.

Looking for a Decision

Jane wants to put potential game-players at the heart of the decision-making process. She has numerous ideas about how best to develop her game, but she can't be sure exactly what will make the difference between people buying it or not. Jane takes great pride in empowering the consumer. They will have the ultimate say.

Jane is seeking a consensus. Those who put the final decision in the hands of their prospective customers focus on finding clear patterns of response. They set aside the thoughts and comments that might cloud an otherwise consistent story and concentrate on those responses that support clear decision-making, over and above minority reservations, concerns and opinions.

Jane's choir sings with one voice.

Sort of.

Composition Bias

Before you ask people what they think, be honest with yourself about your motives for asking. They will define what you seek, how you seek it, how you listen, the illusions you fall for, how you interpret response and the path you choose to take. It is called composition bias.

Don't confuse composition bias with confirmation bias. Confirmation bias is about hearing what you want to hear, for good or for bad. Composition bias is much bigger than that. It's about asking, hearing, processing and decision-making. If you let it, composition bias can and will shape every step of your journey of asking.

Step 1: Your approach to asking
Before you even ask, your motives will influence the way in which you approach the conversation:

- Affirmation: I'm determined to get what I need out of the asking.

- Confidence: I'm both excited and nervous about what people will think of my idea. I hope they like it.

- Insight: I'm keen to explore needs, gather insight and better understand the response.

- Decision: I'm hopeful the results will be clear and consistent. I want answers.

Step 2: The questions you ask

Next, your motives will underpin your every question:

- Affirmation: What do you like about my idea? What are the highlights?

- Confidence: Is my idea any good? Do you like it? What are your reservations?

- Insight: Tell me about the way you play games? How do you really feel about the idea?

- Decision: Do you want my idea? Will you buy it? What would make you want it more?

Step 3: Your approach to listening

Your motives will impact on your ability to listen:

- Affirmation: That's exactly what I thought you would say. What I'm hearing makes perfect sense to me.

- Confidence: I'm glad you like it. But tell me about your niggles and negatives. It sounds like we haven't got this quite right.

- Insight: I'm open to whatever you have to say. Tell me more. Keep going. I'm all ears.

- Decision: I'm on the lookout for coherent themes and dominant perspectives. It's interesting that a few people have made similar comments.

Step 4: The illusions you succumb to

Your motives make you more susceptible to specific illusions:

- Affirmation: Affirmers focus on appeal, overlook what people do, tell to sell, and collude in a shared sense of purpose.

- Confidence: Confidence seekers also focus on appeal (or a lack of it) and readily accept requests for facts and further information.

- Insight: Insight junkies fall for the illusion of interest and get carried away with conversations about personality.

- Decision: Decision-makers avoid thinking about the battles that lie ahead and enthusiastically embrace worthless expressions of desire.

Step 5: Your interpretation of response

Your motives will affect your ability to read a map:

- Affirmation: I was going this direction anyway. I've been proven correct.

- Confidence: I didn't know which way I was going before, and I still don't know.

- Insight: I know where I want to get to, and I have a better understanding of how to get there.

- Decision: I'm going the way I've been told. Isn't that great!

Step 6: The decisions you take

And finally, your motivations for asking will change your direction of travel, or not, as the case may be:

- Affirmation: Carry on regardless.

- Confidence: Tweak, fiddle and procrastinate.

- Insight: Adapt, refine, move on.

- Decision: Go that way.

Calm Your Soul

A planner at the ad agency Saatchi & Saatchi once said to me, 'The best researchers have a calm soul. They listen without agenda. They hear without their own needs or the needs of their clients clouding their mind.'

As the owner of an idea, it is almost impossible to calm your soul and uncloud your mind. It is your prerogative to have a point of view. That's why it pays to employ someone to do the asking for you. Even so, you must be honest with yourself. We make poor decisions based on the opinions of others because we are not prepared to admit our underlying reasons for seeking out those opinions in the first place. We like to believe insight is the driver of asking, that we are open-minded and keen to learn, yet in truth, we hope for a pat on the back, seek reassurance and want to be relieved of our responsibilities.

The hidden motives which filter how we ask, what we hear and what we do are often the chief culprits of insight gone wrong. If you're prepared to be honest with yourself, asking people what they think will reveal more to you about your own relationship with your idea than it will about the thoughts and feelings of the people you have asked. The more willing you are to recognise your real reasons for asking, the more successful the asking will be. Next time you ask, take the ACID test.

19

No Guts No Glory

In 2015 a leading international company with a raft of famous brands commissioned an interesting piece of research. They asked their insight managers across the globe to assess how the brand teams they worked alongside viewed the role of consumer insight as part of the process of advertising development. What approach to research did marketing teams and their ad agency partners believe best contributed to the creation of great ideas?

The organisation in question was unusual because at the time, unlike most corporates, they did not mandate a set approach to consumer research as part of the process of creative development. The global strategic management team provided training and made recommendations based on current best practice, but individual marketing teams retained ultimate responsibility for what type, how much and how often consumer research was commissioned over the course of the development journey.

The conclusions were inconclusive.

At one extreme, a minority of marketing directors fervently believed asking undermined creativity. They looked upon any sort of consumer feedback as interference. At the other end of the scale, several marketing directors wanted creative concepts rigorously tested at every stage of their development. The more closely they consulted the intended audience the better. Most of those interviewed sat somewhere between the two.

The results of the different approaches were similarly mixed. Some of the campaigns created relying solely on the instincts of the team were brilliant. Others completely missed the mark. Equally, some of those ideas tested on multiple occasions during their development were stilted and contrived. Others were a work of genius. There was no obvious right or wrong way. Intuition was not discernibly better or worse than diligently collected consumer insight and performance data.

So, should you rely on your gut instincts when developing your ideas or take on board the opinions of others? Gut or guidance? That is the question.

The answer is: It depends.

Yes, you should trust your gut if you feed it well.

No, you shouldn't trust your gut if you feed it rubbish.

Understanding Intuition

Trusting your gut instincts has become synonymous with ignoring what other people think. Forging your own path. Going it alone. That's a shame, because that definition of intuitive decision-making is based on a complete misunderstanding of how instinct actually works.

Gut instinct is a wonderfully evocative expression for describing how we make choices when we know we don't have all the relevant information at our fingertips. It's another way of saying, 'There are an unfeasibly large number of factors to consider and too many variables outside of my control, so I'm going to have to take responsibility and make a judgement call. To help me do that, I'm going to put everything I know into a big pot, stir it all together, whack in a few bits of experience I've gathered over the years, and go with my gut.'

What appears instinctive is, in fact, the result of a vast array of acquired knowledge and accumulated wisdom blended together to facilitate the making of a fully flavoured decision. Like a lamb tagine. The tastiness of the outcome relies heavily on the quality of the raw ingredients thrown into the pot. When developing ideas designed to meet people's needs, the finest ingredients we have at our disposal are the opinions of those we are trying to impress. Obviously. The extent to which you can trust your instincts depends, therefore, almost entirely on what you choose to do with those opinions.

If you're prepared to make the effort to interpret the feedback and compose truth based on a varied selection of responses, then absolutely, you should trust your gut. On the other hand, if you subscribe to the belief that making intuitive decisions means you don't have to bother with other people's opinions, then relying on your gut instincts is probably a very bad idea. After all, why would you put your faith in a starving gut? Equally, if fuelling your gut instincts involves gulping down concentrated responses, stuffing your face full of unfiltered feedback and surviving on a diet of incomplete and unbalanced compositions, I'd give that a miss as well.

The Working Gut

Making intuitive decisions based on gut instinct is part of our everyday lives. From the trivial – 'With whom shall I spend the rest of my days?' to the more fundamental – 'Should we paint the kids' bedroom Cooking Apple Green or Chelsea Blue?' Through constant and varied use, we know from personal experience whether we make good or bad decisions based on a gut feeling.

At work, we are rarely as self-aware. Because unlike the regularly exercised instincts of ordinary life, our working gut instincts tend to be underused and rusty. Few important decisions at work are made by one person alone. There's always someone else to ask and most employees have a boss who makes the final call. Even if the buck stops with us, the majority of our working hours are spent doing rather than creating. Our professional gut instincts remain underfed and largely unemployed.

Should you need to call on the services of your inactive working gut, my advice is simple: Eat sensibly. Talk to enough people to ensure you get a broad spectrum of response and then work through the Wonder Wheel. In short, cook with good ingredients and chew properly. Whether you choose to consult your consumers often or occasionally, as long as you're willing to figure out what the feedback really means, you'll be surprised how well-nourished your decision-making can become.

The Difficult Second Album

It has often surprised me how common it is for marketing teams to succeed in creating a compelling idea at the first time of asking, yet fail the second time around. Turns out, it's a problem of the gut. If you've had past successes, it's easy to lose sight of how much time, energy and effort was invested in gathering together opinions and understanding response during the process of creative development. In rosy retrospection, it's tempting to believe our good decisions came directly from the mystical depths of our soul and proudly proclaim, 'I didn't listen to what other people were telling me; I trusted my gut.'

Now we know that doesn't make any sense, because listening to opinions and instinct are inextricably entwined. It's just a question of doing the asking well rather than badly. People find it hard to recreate success because they lose the ability to listen with an open mind. They fall for the illusion of interest and shift their motive for asking from insight to affirmation. Conversely, those who go on to succeed time and time again never lose sight of what having faith in their instincts really involves. They know that including the opinions of others in the process of developing their ideas doesn't make them any the less brilliant; it simply allows them to add the qualities of perception, empathy, providence and understanding to the being brilliant list.

Models and Maps

Part One of this book is about understanding response. Part Two is about the truth. Both are underpinned by a shared philosophy – the principle of inevitable uncertainty. When you ask for feedback, there are only two guarantees:

1. Response is flawed

2. People cannot be trusted

The solution in both cases is to embrace the inevitable. As soon we are prepared to accept the reality, we can begin to put in place the strategies and interventions that will enable us to navigate our way through unpredictable lands. To support us on our journey, we have a model and a map. The model improves our understanding of response. The map helps us to compose truth.

Sitting as we do, at the centre of the world of asking, our first task as composer is to gather together the supporter, developer, critic and disinterested. Then we can begin to compose. Next, we should take the ACID test. Good composition demands that we acknowledge our motivations for asking, for without self-awareness we are compromised composers. And finally, we should trust our gut instincts. Assuming, of course, we understand what trusting our gut actually entails. When it comes to feeding our instincts, we have three choices:

1. Starve ourselves of insight and understanding

2. Gorge ourselves on rubbish

3. Source good ingredients, prepare them well and eat with care. Then stick to the habits that made us fit and strong.

Choose Option Three for a healthy and prosperous future.

END OF PART TWO

Part Three

GOOD ASKING GUIDE

'Travelling, one accepts everything;
indignation stays at home'
Elias Canetti, The Voices of Marrakesh

Introduction
to the Guide

Think of this as the basic information every traveller needs for their journey to the land of asking. It includes practical advice, recommendations, hints and tips to help you get the most out of the experience. The guide has seven sections:

1. Back to Basics

2. The Good Traveller

3. What to Pack

4. Where to Stay

5. Learning the Language

6. Keeping Out of Trouble

7. The Golden Triangle

The advice is equally relevant for a dating app, wearable tech, cake decorations or board games. The same lessons apply whether asking online or in-person and should be as helpful to the amateur asker as they are to a professional market researcher. Take heed and you'll have a great time.

1

Back to Basics

Even the loftiest of mountains
begins on the ground
Moroccan proverb [17]

Success in the world of asking rests upon three numbers: one, two and twelve. These three numbers form the unshakeable foundations upon which you can begin to construct your understanding and compose your truth.

One

One person and their opinion is the basic building block of asking. Without the individual members of our choir, we have no choir. And without the one, there is no wonder.

The world of asking is a place where every individual must be respected and valued. As the question asker, it is our responsibility to connect with, listen to, embolden and celebrate the individual perspectives that contribute to our overall composition.

The first rule of travelling is this: Every individual you ask must have their own discernible identity. That is non-negotiable. If you cannot name the person you are asking, don't ask them what they think. After all, why would you entrust your idea to someone you don't even know exists?

Mistaken Identity

There are issues of identity in the world of asking. It is not unheard of for regular attendees of research groups to pretend to be someone they are not. Groups often include an over-representation of out-of-work artists, actors and wannabe stand-up comedians – all of whom spend too much time on their own, enjoy role play and need the cash.

'Today, Jon, my name is Gary, I mean Sylvia. I live in Reading with my husband, Sylvia, I mean Gary, and I like buying premium quality hi-fi, feminine hygiene products and continental car tyres.'

If you are doing the asking yourself, seeing the face of your respondent is the simplest way of ensuring the person you are talking to is genuinely who they say they are. If you commission a research agency to conduct the interviews on your behalf, ask them about the steps they have taken to ensure the quality of recruitment. Either way, if you intend to make decisions about the future of your idea based on individual opinions, you must have confidence in the identity of those you are asking.

Multiple Mistaken Identities

Here's a question for you: Have you ever met someone, either personally or professionally, who completes market research surveys for cash? I haven't.

If you were to sign up to one of the many online market research panels offering rewards for opinions, you would be paid, on average, £1 per survey. Typically, payment is made via a shopping voucher after a number of surveys have been completed. I ask you: Would any of your customers be willing to spend hours of their time filling in surveys for a £10 voucher? I doubt it.

Before you commission a survey, find out how much potential participants are being paid. Be honest with yourself. Would you take part for that amount of money? Is your ideal customer the type of person who would happily complete an online survey for little or no reward? And if your sample is supposed to be representative of the wider population, why are they filling out surveys? I'm all for asking. Ask away. But ask real people, not impersonators. Otherwise, it's a waste of your time and money. If you cannot guarantee the identity of the people you are asking, your composition is constructed on foundations of popsicle sticks and rubber cement.[18]

Two

Now we know who we are talking to, we can concentrate on getting the most out of each and every person we ask. Let's start with you. If you were being asked for your opinion, what would you want the experience of asking to be like? What would ease your path to telling the truth?

The answer is simple. We feel most able to express ourselves in the company of people we know and trust. In the presence of good friends and loved ones, our default is to tell the truth. Surrounded by close friends and family, research participants do not feel compelled to agree or disagree with each other. There is no self-consciousness or sense of inadequacy. Diverse experiences and feelings are not only accepted, they are positively encouraged.

Friendship and family pairs form the foundations of honest response. Online or face to face, talk to people who know each other.

Of course, there may be times when it is preferable to ask people on their own or in a group. For example, one to one interviews are often more suitable for delicate subjects and off the cuff conversations. But bear in mind, depth interviews do not necessarily mean deeper insight. Paradoxically, it is often harder for people to be themselves when they are on their own. The less confident find it particularly difficult to open up when flying solo.

Focus groups, on the other hand, are more traditionally associated with the development of creative concepts.

The group dynamic supposedly encourages participants to bounce ideas off each other. But the notion that research groups generate a greater diversity of response and facilitate creativity is a myth. Two good friends are just as likely to have differing opinions as a group of strangers picked at random. Crucially, however, they find it easier to say what they really think. And it is the freedom to express themselves without inhibition that provides the catalyst for true creativity. Conversely, amongst strangers, the less vocal soon lose confidence and retire into their shells. Those with differing perspectives become reluctant to express their inner feelings for fear of setting themselves up as adversaries. Ideas developed amongst people who don't know each other are far more likely to be safe and mediocre. Groups and greatness rarely go hand in hand.

Furthermore, the happy chatter of a focus group should never be confused with truth. The clue is in the name. *Focus* groups are the perfect breeding ground for the illusion of interest.

Talking in pairs is not intended as an absolute. It's a start point and a principle. The priority is to ensure the environment for asking encourages honesty and openness. If you speak to people on their own, be kind and sensitive. Should you feel the need to run a focus group, construct it out of friendship pairs – three sets of pairs maximum. Never talk to more than six people at a time. It becomes a tiresome exercise in turn-waiting, swallowed instincts and holding back.

Twelve

Juries have been made up of twelve men and women, good and true, for over 800 years.

Whilst the original rationale for the jury of twelve is not entirely clear, the foremost reason for the enduring appeal of the number twelve is beautifully simple. Within any group of twelve individuals there is always room for dissent. Get a dozen people in a room and at least one will have a different perspective to everyone else. If all twelve can come to a unanimous verdict, you have greater certainty the correct decision has been made.

For similar reasons, twelve people also constitute the firm foundation for good composition. Within every set of twelve respondents, you should encounter a mix of supporters, developers, critics and the disinterested. Twelve well-chosen people will enable you to make wise judgements rooted in a sound understanding of how your consumers feel about your idea. Amazing but true.

There are, however, four vital differences between a jury of law and your choir of composition:

1. The choir doesn't decide the direction of your idea. You do. You are the composer.

2. You're not looking for unanimity or even a majority. In fact, you want the exact opposite. The aim is to gather together a diverse range of responses. That's why twelve works so well.

3. All twelve of your choir members must be representative of your target audience. Unlike a real jury, you don't want to talk to twelve people selected at random. If your aim is to develop affordable dishwasher tablets, there's no point in talking to people who don't own dishwashers.

4. Nobody is going to jail.

Multiples of Twelve

If you need to establish how different regions of the country feel about your idea, talk to twelve in each. If you suspect there may be significant differences between potential customers who have children and those who do not, talk to twelve of each. If you seek the truth in London, Paris and New York, talk to twelve in each. And so on.

How Can Twelve Be Enough? I Need More Robust Data.

Businesses large and small make investment decisions based on the performance of an idea in consumer testing. The assumption is that the data used for decision-making is sound. It is not. The response of one thousand anonymous souls online is no more real than a conversation with a random stranger in a pub. The large numbers form a facade.

Data can only be truly robust if it is based on actual performance and real behaviour. Real sales data. Real click-through data. Real service experiences. When you ask people what they think of an idea the response is never real, no matter how many people you ask. Using large sample sizes to assess the potential of an idea is simply a more defensible way of handing over the keys to the car. It has nothing to do with robustness. Making decisions about the ongoing development of creative ideas based on survey results may look like good business practice, but it's a cop-out.

Rather than rely on large numbers of people you don't know and will never meet, ask twelve people what they think, ask them why they think it and based on their feedback compose your truth. That may sound unsettling, but only because the onus is on you. The quality of your decision-making and the resulting success of your idea will depend almost entirely on your ability to interpret the response and the beauty of your composition. If you're not convinced, ask yourself these two questions:

Question 1: Have I spoken to enough people to give me a clear steer on the direction I should take?

Answer: Why are you letting your respondents drive?

Question 2: Have I spoken to enough people to gather together a mix of supportive, developmental, critical and disinterested responses?

Answer: Yes.

Testing, Testing, One Two, One Two

Individual people with individual names and individual faces form the bedrock of the land of asking. Assuming your respondents meet these basic requirements, your main concern must be to create a context for asking in which it is easier for people to tell the truth than it is to lie. When research participants are in the company of those they know and trust, the characteristics of asking are less demanding, the instructions of the game more transparent, the subtext less hidden, there is less holding back, and tongues are less sore. Finally, your goal should be to gather together enough people to ensure you have the full set of voices in your choir. So, start with twelve and build from there.

2

The Good Traveller

Nothing is true, all is permissible

Moroccan proverb

As every experienced traveller knows, the more effort you make to immerse yourself in the culture of the country you are visiting, the more you will get out of your trip. The following ten rules of engagement should help you to forge a closer and more productive relationship with the locals in the land of asking.

1. Be interested. There is nothing so powerful as being interested in what people have to say. It's rare for someone to truly care about our opinion. We like it. We open up. Your aim should be to create a safe space where all responses are welcome. Of course, you don't have to trust every opinion expressed, but you do have to make sure everyone you ask believes you genuinely

care about what they have to say. That will be easy, because you do.

2. Celebrate honesty. People need to know you value truth. As the question asker, they will automatically assume you are also, at least to some degree, the idea owner – and they may well be right. The instinct of those you are asking will be to play the part of the good respondent rather than say what they really think. Explain that your only concern is the truth. You don't mind what they say, as long as their response truly reflects how they feel. Make it explicitly clear there are no right or wrong answers. And don't rush. People are naturally closed. They tend to be reluctant to reveal their true feelings. Be patient, interested and encouraging. When someone tells you what they really think, thank them for their honesty.

3. Ask with an open mind. Respondents are made of litmus paper. They will know if you are looking for a particular response. When clients come to research sessions, I always encourage them to get involved. It's striking how often the questions they ask give the game away. People are not stupid. Agendas are always transparent. Even online. Calm your soul and for the duration of time you spend in the land of asking, make insight your goal.

4. Be broad-minded about people's ability to express themselves insightfully. You can't guess from looking at someone how valuable their response will be. Respondents have an endless capacity to surprise.

5. Be led by listening. If you listen properly, the conversation will flow. You'll be able to explore everything you want to know about your idea in the context of this natural conversation. Listen to what people say and follow their train of thought. Forcing someone to go one way or another implies you are looking for a specific answer. Remember, when people respond in a way that doesn't seem relevant, you're catching a glimpse of the real world. Confused, self-centred, even pointless responses are part of the journey. You are far better off driving down an honest conversation cul-de-sac than speeding down the highway of delusion.

6. Embrace contradiction. Often people start off saying one thing and contradict themselves later. Notice it, but don't pick them up on it. It's not a good idea to make people feel self-conscious. It's your job to work out which is more important: the initial instinctive opinion or the more considered response.

7. Be nice. It's hard not to become frustrated when people don't answer in the way you want them to, but nothing inhibits response more than annoyance. If the person you are asking suspects you are frustrated by their answer, they will either clam up or aim to please. Neither is productive. Be kind, sensitive and encouraging.

8. Don't dismiss the disinterested. It is oh so tempting to be guided by the responses of the super-engaged. The discussion with people who care about your

idea, business or brand, is always more fun than the conversation with those who do not. But if your aim is to convert the unconvinced, the thoughts of the disinterested and detached are invaluable.

9. Be realistic. Sometimes asking doesn't work out, and that's okay. People are people. If your goal is good composition and you seek insight rather than answers, you will be more sanguine about the experience of asking. In turn, you will be calmer in your approach, your questions will be more open, you will listen harder and learn more.

10. Enjoy yourself. Asking people what they think should be an enlightening, educational and growing experience. Remember, it's a serious business for you, but it's a game for your respondents. Keep it light. Gathering feedback should be the most enjoyable part of the development process. It's when your idea becomes real. If you don't get a kick out of mixing with the locals and seeing how they respond to your idea, don't get on the magic carpet.

3

What to Pack

Little and lasting is better than much and passing

Moroccan proverb

When you ask people what they think, your ideas will often be half-formed at best. By definition, early-stage concepts, innovations, scripts, wireframes, prototypes and partially developed ideas are a poor representation of the finished article and will almost certainly need some explaining.

Before you start asking, you must, therefore, decide what to show and how much to describe. It's a balance. On the one hand, there's no point asking people to give their opinion about something that bears no relation to your intended idea, and on the other, telling is selling.

When it comes to developing stimulus – the materials you use to present your idea – it's impossible to be definitive.

Every idea is different, and there are so many points in the development process at which you could turn to people for feedback that a best practice, one-size-fits-all solution to stimulus becomes meaningless.

My advice is to travel light.

As anyone who has ever packed a suitcase knows, that is easier said than done. Hopefully, the following four tips will help:

1. Do your idea justice. If you don't have confidence in your stimulus or feel that it misrepresents your idea, you'll find it hard to embrace the response.

2. Keep everything to an absolute minimum. The more you frame your idea, the less reliable the response becomes. Cut out any fluff. Use as few images and words as possible to bring your idea to life. Excess baggage will cost you dearly.

3. Don't be precious. Outline ideas and rough-drawn images often prove to be better stimulus than well-polished concepts. Respondents tend to regard rudimentary stimulus as work in progress and find it easier to respond conceptually as a result. Conversely, the more refined the stimulus, the more likely people are to get hung up on small executional details. If you are in the final stages of development, that may be fine. But earlier in the process, discussions about the details of your drawing and the specifics of your description are invariably a distraction.

4. If the tools you are using to represent your idea are consistently sending people down the wrong track, you're better off changing the stimulus than trying to redirect the conversation. The more you re-explain your idea, the more likely you are to be selling rather than asking. It will soon become apparent if your stimulus is wrong, and the best thing you can do is repack and start again.

Finally, have faith. Trust your respondents. Get your idea out there and see what people think. Needing to adapt and flex the way in which you present your concept is part of the process of learning. Refining your stimulus as you travel will only be problematic if you are looking for a concrete answer, desperately seeking a winner or hoping for a pat on the back.

4

Where to Stay

A garden without a fence is like
a dog without a tail

Moroccan proverb

Where you do your asking is an important consideration. Aside from the entire world falling apart, one of the consequences of COVID-19 has been the rapid adoption of video conferencing as part of our everyday life. Over the last few years, asking has been increasingly moving online and the step change in the use of video calling prompted by the pandemic has only served to guarantee its place as the future home of asking. That having been said, there are pros and cons to interviewing online or in-person. For example, online conversations tend to lack the nuance and richness of insight to be gleaned from physically being in the same space as your respondents. Yet they also avoid some of the undue influence that inevitably accompanies researcher and respondent sitting in the same room. In these changing times, only one thing is certain; there will always be a role for both.

The key, therefore, is not to think in terms of online versus in-person research, but to focus first and foremost on the participant experience. Your only concern should be to make sure their involvement is as pleasant and relaxed as possible. To which end, whether you choose to chat virtually or meet with your respondents in the flesh, my advice remains the same.

1. Formal research environments lead to formal responses. If you ask people to download dedicated research software to take part in a discussion, the response will not be as natural as it would be via Zoom. Similarly, a chat over coffee at the kitchen table will elicit a more honest and intuitive response than the same conversation around a boardroom table in a sterile hotel conference room. Often the needs of the research team determine the methodology chosen for research, rather than those of the respondent. Convenience is promoted over comfort and process is prioritised above people. That is the wrong way around. Respondents' needs come first.

2. There's a 9 pm curfew on asking people what they think. After nine-o-clock, people are either brain dead or drunk.

3. On the subject of drink, stay away from the minibar. Only offer your respondents tea, coffee and soft drinks, particularly if you are talking to children.

4. Don't overstay your welcome. Depending on how much you have to talk about, asking should last between five and sixty minutes. Informal asking tends to be fast. People are not interested in looking at multiple ideas and explaining themselves in detail. If you are having an off the cuff conversation about your idea, ask the person what they think, ask them why they think it, and then move on. In a dedicated research environment, you have longer to play – for better and for worse. But you still only have one hour, max. If you need to talk to people for more than sixty minutes, you are:

- Testing too many ideas
- Talking to too many people at once
- Being self-indulgent
- All the above

Attention spans have shortened over recent years and the days of extended two-hour research groups have long gone. Online or face-to-face, you would be better served running multiple short sessions of friendship pairs rather than a small number of bloated group discussions chock full of strangers. If you are talking to pairs of friends, you don't need to warm your respondents up. You can quickly cut to the chase, gather your guests' opinions and let them be on their way.

5

Learning the Language

Let us sit bent, but talk straight

Moroccan proverb

The language of asking is easily learnt.
There are only six rules:

Rule number one:
If you have a question to ask, ask it. Don't beat around
the bush. Ask away.

Rule number two:
Don't be the idiot that forgot to ask why.

It's perfectly normal to probe as part of a conversation. So, if you don't fully understand the answer, ask why.

Why do you say that?
Could you explain?
What do you mean?
Help me understand?

But be careful. Make it clear your follow-up questions are borne out of a desire to better understand the response, rather than an expression of your eagerness for a different type of answer. Be aware that any additional questions are likely to magnify the illusion of interest. And remember, asking people to analyse their instinctive response is fraught with danger. Reservations aside, if you don't ask why, you simply won't be able to gather together the complete set of responses you require to take your responsibilities seriously. Better to ask why and make the effort to interpret the answer than not to ask and never know.

Rule number three: Listen.

The most common mistake we make when asking for feedback is to forget to listen. Often, we fail to hear properly because valuable head space is being taken up worrying about the next question. Listening is impossible if you have too many questions buzzing around inside your brain. You need to relax. Rest assured, you know the questions you want to ask, it's the answers you don't have. Concentrate on listening and the right questions will come.

Rule number four: Don't fret about the way you ask.

Clearly, open questions are better than closed questions. All things being equal, 'What do you think of my idea?' should elicit more valuable insight than 'Do you like my idea?' The former opens up the possibility of good composition and the latter closes it down. But intonation and expression also play their part. 'What don't you like about my idea?' and 'Why didn't you like it, you little shit?' are both open questions, but one is more likely to prompt a helpful response than the other. A closed question asked in an open-minded way will be far more productive than an open question underpinned by the sense of a right or wrong answer. If you are genuinely interested in what people have to say, the way you ask the question will be fine. On the other hand, if you have an agenda, it doesn't matter how you ask the question. Open or closed, your respondents will know you have an answer in mind.

Rule numbe ..... don't interrupt. (You see what I did there?) If you shut down response, you are, in effect, telling your respondent you don't value what they have to say. Apart from a grimace and a loud sigh, nothing indicates your dissatisfaction more obviously than interruption.

Rule number six: Leave some space for silence

Body Language

Language is not confined to words. Whether you're in the same room as your respondents or chatting via video, you need to watch as well as listen. Bear in mind, observed responses can be deceptive. You can never predict with any great certainty what is going on inside someone's head from their facial movements and physical reactions. And try not to be distracted by a smiley face. A happy reaction is as likely to be a sign of comfortable familiarity as it is to be a symbol of success. Nevertheless, in the peculiar world of asking, there are a couple of tell-tale non-verbal signals it is worth keeping a particular eye on.

The first is the sideways glance. When talking to two or more people at the same time, if one of your respondents gives another a quick look before they speak, it's a sure-fire sign they are editing their opinion for approval. Edited responses are no good to you. Encourage the glancer to reveal their first instincts. Gently remind them there is no such thing as a right or wrong answer. All you care about is their honest opinion and personal point of view.

Secondly, if your respondent is sitting back with folded arms and crossed legs, they are almost certainly defending themselves against you and your intrusive questions. Their guarded responses will be neither intuitive nor a true reflection of what they genuinely think. You need to find a way to break down their defences. Whether online or in person, try this simple two-step technique:

Step one

Slowly and deliberately mirror their defensive body language. Sit back in your chair. Sit upright. Fold your arms. Then cross your legs.

Step two

Unguard one part of your body at a time. Don't rush and keep eye contact. Bend your back. Lean forward. Unfold your arms, and finally, uncross your legs. Hopefully, your respondent will start to unfurl and you, in turn, can begin to believe what they say. I can't guarantee it will work, but the fact you are so mindful of and attentive to their non-verbal communication will stand your in good stead.

That's all there is to it. I promised asking is easy, and it is. There is nothing complicated about the language of asking. Sit bent, talk straight, job done.

6

Keeping Out of Trouble

The camel never sees his own hump, but that
of his brother is always in his eyes

Moroccan proverb

Like the illusion of interest, influence is inevitable. When
you ask people what they think, every opinion expressed
will immediately and unavoidably influence those who hear
it. The same is true of ideas. Seeing one iteration of an idea
will automatically affect the way people feel about the next.
Yet, unlike the pesky illusions that populate the land of
asking, influence also occurs naturally in the real world. It
is normal for us to seek out the opinions of others before
we make decisions and we regularly compare products to
improve the quality of the choices we make.

Whilst you do not, therefore, need to be overly afraid of influence, you do need to take it seriously. It is important to recognise when and how responses have been influenced and take the appropriate action to minimise the danger. For without proper attention, undue influence can and will lead you astray. So, keep your wits about you and be on alert for the following types of influence:

1. Domination

2. Expertise

3. Education

4. Relativity

As well as being the composer of truth, you are also the conductor of the choir. Your job is to enable everyone you ask to find their true voice. You don't want to stop anyone from singing, but when you witness excessive interference, it is your responsibility to calm things down. So, dust off your tuxedo, grab hold of your baton and keep your eyes peeled. By conducting with sensitivity and awareness, your choir will thank you and express their gratitude through their unadulterated opinions.

Domination

When you talk to two or more people together, one person will often try to dominate the discussion. If given free rein, they'll answer every question first and attempt to direct the conversation. You can't afford to let that happen. It is vital that all your respondents have the opportunity to express their instinctive opinions.

Use your hands to conduct the choir.

Should the same person constantly try to answer first, give them the stop sign.

Do it gently, but assertively. Dominant respondents tend to know they talk too much, so if you manage them correctly, you won't offend, and they will get the message. Make sure your actions don't inadvertently suggest you're looking for a particular response. Your aim is to nip influence in the bud, not shut people down. So, give dominant respondents the hand before they start speaking rather than mid-sentence. Once they get going, you should let them finish.

Keep in mind, the need to speak first and speak often is not the same as the need to be right. Big-mouthed does not necessarily mean narrow-minded, nor does outward confidence always equate to inner belief. Despite being noisy, dominant respondents frequently need encouragement to reveal their true thoughts. Conversely, if given a chance to speak, the seemingly shy participant will often turn out to be assertive and assured.

Try to sense when someone at the back of the choir has something to say. To those politely waiting their turn, beckon them forward.

Indicate through your actions that it is their time to talk. Never underestimate the importance of demonstrating to quieter respondents that their thoughts and feelings are important to you. By drawing forward the reticent, you will be richly rewarded.

Expertise

When asked for feedback, it is only natural for respondents to defer to those they believe to be better informed. For example, what do you think of this ad encouraging dog owners to clear up their dog mess?[19]

Do you need to be a parent to have a point of view? No, of course you don't. Would it help if you worked in marketing? No. Would it make a difference if you were an expert in public health? Certainly not. In fact, your closeness to the subject would probably get in the way of your ability to respond instinctively. How about a first class honours degree. Would that help? No. What if you've got

lots of money, live in a big house and drive a Tesla? Would that make a difference? No. A judge? No. How about being blind? Now you're being silly. What about owning a dog? Yup. That would be good. Does it need to be a specific breed? Stop it.

As you can see, there are endless ways in which one respondent could claim expertise over another and numerous opportunities for participants to defer to those they think know better. Despite dog mess being a universally relevant message, those without children would almost certainly wait for parents to speak first and, depending on the response, revise their opinions accordingly. There is no reason why they should, but they would.

Whether you are talking about football, finance or phones, there is always someone in the room who knows more, is closer to the subject and believes they are a better judge. And less knowledgeable respondents will instinctively turn to them for help. Yet the expert and interested are only ever going to represent a tiny proportion of your intended audience. Usually, your goal will be to convert the unconvinced. You must make sure the less well-informed also have ample opportunity to speak their mind.

The best way to manage the influence of expertise is to name it. Endorse ignorance from the outset. Start the conversation by reassuring your respondents what they don't know is as important to you as what they do. Acknowledge that some people know more about interest rates and work-out routines than others, and that's okay. Be explicit. Explain the whole point of asking is to understand different perspectives. All opinions are equally important. Spell out that it is fine to be influenced by others, but you want to hear and understand their personal instincts and uninformed responses first.

Education

Over the course of being asked for their opinion, respondents acquire a depth of knowledge about an idea they would not otherwise have known. To experience this process of education in action, we need to return to Chapter 1 and put ourselves in the shoes of teenage dad Finn and his former sexual partner Hailey, mother of his child.[20]

Lesson One: Pants
Have a look at this rough ad and see what you think.

There's something interesting about the idea, isn't there? Intuitively, the concept seems strong. But it's difficult to know what to think just from one poster. Rather than get carried away, perhaps we should reserve judgement until we see another.

Lesson Two: Tosser

Here's a second poster. What do you think?

Now we're getting somewhere. It's an excellent ad.

Why don't we take the Wonder Wheel for a spin and break the response down?

Appeal: The fingers are funny and clever.

Purpose: It's about being in control.

Relevance: As a seventeen-year-old, it talks my language.

Impact: I'd definitely notice it.

Clarity: The message is clear. No condom, no sex.

Belief: I can imagine a girl saying that.

Personality: I like the edgy, straight-talking tone.

Desire: The idea certainly has potential. Although, I'm not convinced how much difference it will make in the heat of the moment.

Lesson Three: Radio

Have a read of the radio ad:

> Girl: So he's got everything...
> Boy: The face, the body...
> Girl: The clothes, the cool...
> Boy: The eyes, the class...
> Girl: He's hot...
> Boy: She's a honey...
> Girl: But he didn't have condoms.
> Boy: I don't use condoms, babe.
> Girl: So how many 'babes' has he had?
> Boy: Don't like 'em, don't need 'em.
> Girl: Well, I do.
> Boy: You want to think yourself lucky, girl...
> Girl: You know what?
> Boy: What?
> Girl: I do.
> Boy (*bitter*): Her loss, eh?
> Girl (*disappointed*): His loss.
> Female voice-over: Want respect? Use a condom.

Ah, now I get it. The penny has dropped. The individual ads about contraception are part of a wider message of empowerment under the banner of self-respect. The aim is not merely to encourage young men and women to take precautions, but more importantly, to respect their bodies. I like it.

Lesson Four: Respect

Finally, what do you think of the logo?

It's clever, isn't it? The condom is creatively incorporated into both the campaign identity and the message of love and respect.

All in all, it's a well-constructed campaign, each of the separate elements contributing to the communication of an overarching message, more powerful and meaningful than the sum of its parts.

The trouble is the response to everything other than the first poster is based on an increasingly enriched understanding of how the campaign works. We have accumulated an unrealistic depth of knowledge over the course of the asking, and our response to the individual executions cannot therefore be trusted.

The same is true of anything we might test, be it products, policies, programmes, websites, apps, etcetera. As we explore response, discuss feelings, and layer on features and benefits, we educate our respondents and change the response. The more our respondents see, read and hear, the less reliable the response becomes.

Of course, if you explore every element of your idea separately, you avoid the problem. But breaking asking down into bite-sized chunks is rarely practical. Nor is it necessarily the right thing to do. After all, if people only read Chapter 1 of your book, how can you find out what they think of the whole story. In the real world, products and services are made up of multiple moving parts, and marketing campaigns are designed to work as a collective. Furthermore, comparing different executions of the same idea is an invaluable way of exploring their relative merits – more of which in a moment.

The solution, as ever, is down to you. Rather like Finn and Hailey, you're going to have to take responsibility for your own actions. You need to recognise that the more you show, the more distorted the response will become. Every illusion will be magnified exponentially. As the influence grows, the harder you will have to work to see the response for what it truly is. To remain steadfast in the face of an ever-expanding illusion of interest, hold tight to the Wonder Wheel. Use it not simply as a guide to help you ask the right questions, but as the framework for interpreting response.

Relativity

Behavioural scientists use the term relativity to describe the effects of comparing one idea against another. In his book *Predictably Irrational*, Dan Ariely explains how we make decisions based on comparisons. We may not always know what is best, but we know which of the choices available to us we consider to be better. We look at our decisions in a relative way.[21]

Ariely uses a promotional ad for *The Economist* to demonstrate how the presence of multiple ideas influences the choices we make. Of these three subscription options for *The Economist*, which would you choose?

1. Web subscription $59
2. Print subscription $125
3. Print and web subscription $125

The option to buy the print-only version of *The Economist* at the same price as the joint print and web subscription is a pointless choice. But it acts as a decoy. When Ariely asked MIT students which option they would choose, 84% picked option three. Yet when he took away option 2 – the decoy – only 32% chose the print and web option.

Behavioural economics teaches us that humans rarely choose things in absolute terms. Rather, we focus on the relative advantage of one thing over another and estimate value accordingly. We can't tell whether the web-only option at $59 is good value, whereas we know for certain that buying option three is a better deal than buying option two for the same money. The mere presence of the print-only subscription influences the choices made.

Relativity plays an important part in our lives. It allows us to compare apples and pears, make difficult choices and simplify complex decisions. Whether we are buying a house, a bread-maker, or a TV – all examples Ariely uses to demonstrate relativity – the presence of alternative options and the order in which we place those options influence the choices we make.

The same is true of ideas and response. Show three posters, and your respondents will form opinions about their relative merits. As the question asker, you want that to happen. The comparison helps your respondents better understand how they feel about each execution and provides them with the tools to express those feelings. It is easier to explain why you prefer one idea over another than it is to talk about an idea that sits in splendid isolation. And if the response changes depending on the order in which the executions are presented, it affords you the opportunity to learn more about your idea from every angle. Yet, the conversation is artificial. In the real world, people would never see different iterations of the same product side by side. Nor would one part of a campaign be immediately followed by another, without interruption, competition or distraction. Relativity in market research is simultaneously an important tool for understanding and a dangerous mis-representation of our real-world experience.

It Takes Two to Tango

There are two solutions to the problem of relativity. One is practical, the other is a matter of principle.

Firstly, the practical. Rotating the order in which you show your ideas will give you both a true sense of your respondents' feelings toward each idea and allow you to explore their relative merits. By swapping which idea you show first, you get a clean read on the individual execution before you go on to consider comparative responses.

Rotation is another reason why you should work with pairs. It comes down to basic maths. If you ask four groups, with six people in each group, you only have four chances to rotate the order in which your ideas are shown. If you take the same twenty-four people and ask them in pairs, you have twelve opportunities to mix things up.

Moreover, because your respondents know each other, they're happier to reveal their honest feelings from the get-go. In groups, the order effect is generally more marked. Ideas shown first and third tend to suffer when tested with groups of strangers. For the first idea, research participants are finding their feet and checking out their fellow group members. Consequently, they edit, filter and hold back. By the time they get to the third idea, respondents become increasingly analytical. Emotional reactions are abandoned in favour of considered answers and clever suggestions. If you want to better manage the influence of relativity, stick to pairs.

Delusion Before Decoy

There is a force at work in the world of asking far more powerful than the concepts of relativity and 'the decoy'. That force is the illusion of interest. The real trick with *The Economist* experiment is the assumption that research participants are being offered a credible choice in the first place. Asking the question gives the impression that MIT students are desperately keen to buy *The Economist*. Yet, the highest-selling magazines for students in the US are *Cosmopolitan, GQ* and *Sports Illustrated*. Maybe MIT undergraduates are different. I suspect not. The actual percentage of MIT students with a subscription to *The Economist* is probably far closer to zero than 32%. Let alone 84%.

Relativity in market research exaggerates the illusion of interest. We compare one expression of our idea versus another, marvel at the insight and cheer at the result. But we forget we've been duped and deluded. It's predictably irrational. The best way to stay out of trouble is to remember you are not looking for a winner. That is the principle that will keep you safe. If you focus on performance and end up in dog mess, you've only got yourself to blame.

Taking Precautions

You can't do anything about influence in the world of asking. And in some respects, you wouldn't want to – because it's normal. But that doesn't mean you shouldn't take precautions. Good asking requires that you put in place coping strategies and behave in a way that allows you to mitigate the effects of undue influence. That way, you'll be able to have all the fun of asking, without the nasty surprise nine months down the line.

When you want to ask people what they think, respect your respondents but most importantly, respect yourself. Take responsibility for your own actions. Before you expend too much energy worrying about the various ways in which people can influence each other, it's worth remembering the greatest source of influence is likely to be the person asking the questions. In other words, you.

7

The Golden Triangle

'In a tropical landscape one's eye takes in
everything except the human beings'
Marrakesh by George Orwell

Quantitative research is a democracy. Irrespective of how
many people you ask, every answer carries equal weight:
One person, one vote. Our world of asking is based on a
radically different philosophy. It is a meritocracy. To coin
a phrase: All responses are equal, but some are more equal
than others. If you're hoping for everyone to sing from the
same hymn sheet, you've missed the point. Being able to
appreciate the responses that matter most is an essential
part of any visit to the land of asking.

The Golden Triangle of Intelligent Response

While the wonders of asking are best explored with the help of a wheel, the highlights of response can be found within a triangle: The golden triangle of intelligent response.

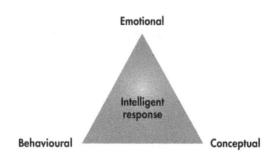

At each of the three points of the triangle sits a different type of intelligence:

1. Emotional

2. Behavioural

3. Conceptual

The last lesson on our journey is this: If you want to make good decisions based on other people's opinions, you can't beat an intelligent response. Spotting the feedback that has any or all three of these intelligent characteristics is critical to the development of compelling ideas.

Emotional Intelligence

'What do you think?' is a rational request. Consequently, the response tends to be thought through rather than instinctive. Many respondents take pride in their rational response. They like to believe the choices they make in the real world are based on facts. Rational respondents will try to pull you back to the ordinary, everyday and predictable.

Emotionally intelligent respondents, on the other hand, are more in touch with their intuitive response. They also have the ability to discern between different feelings and label their emotional responses appropriately. All three skills are important. To be emotionally intelligent in the world of asking, you must feel first rather than think first, and then be able to identify and articulate those feelings.

Emotionally intelligent respondents will help you develop ideas that connect with your audience on a deeper, more visceral level. An emotionally intelligent world includes disabled hedgehogs, politically active red squirrels, over-generous salad carts, perfectly cooked chicken breasts and strawberry mojitos. Well-expressed intuitive responses are highlights you wouldn't want to miss.

Behavioural Intelligence

Behaviourally intelligent responses are grounded in what people do. As we know only too well, being behaviourally intelligent is far from straightforward. Our memories are selective and we are poor witnesses of our own behaviour. Nonetheless, it is occasionally possible for people to recall their recent behaviours in a way that is sincere, honest and valid. For example, I know what I had for breakfast this morning before taking my pet tortoise out for a ten-mile run. And yes, it was freezing.

Behaviourally intelligent respondents automatically put your idea into the context of their lives. They self-start with 'do' so that you don't have to.

In a behaviourally intelligent world, smokers ignore health warnings, the public dismiss political promises, homeowners lay artificial grass in their gardens, football fans watch Manchester United vs Liverpool, and young people get drunk on Saturday night and have unprotected sex. Behaviourally intelligent responses open our eyes to what is really going on and force us to develop relevant ideas that work.

Conceptual Intelligence

Conceptually intelligent respondents can make the leap from concept to concrete. They intuitively respond to an idea as a whole, rather than getting hung up on small executional details. The conceptually intelligent don't take things literally. They understand that rough edges make for distinctive ideas in the real world.

Developers often think of themselves as conceptually intelligent. But having an opinion on how to change a concept is not the same as being able to look past the detail and see an idea's underlying purpose and potential. Conceptually intelligent respondents celebrate creativity, resolve complexity and focus our minds on the battles that must be won. They can even remind us of our true purpose and save us from disaster.

In a conceptually intelligent world, Paralympians can be superhuman. And yet, in 2012, only one respondent had the ability to see past their dislike of the 'Superhumans' campaign stimulus, set aside their natural resistance to ideas that challenge the status quo, and grasp the power of the concept hidden within.

Conceptual intelligence is a superpower.

Singing a Song of Success

All responses are not equal. When we ask people what they think, merit is what matters, not mouth. One thought well expressed, one experience, one trivial aside or one comment can show us the way.

The opinions that matter most are to be found within the golden triangle of intelligent response. Emotionally, behaviourally and conceptually intelligent respondents are your soloists. Hearken to their voices and shower your ideas with their song.

Le Jardin Marjorelle

'A visit to Marrakesh was a great shock to me.
This city taught me color.'

Yves Saint Laurent

The golden triangle of Marrakesh is formed from the locations of three historic sights - the Badi Palace, the Saadian Tombs and the Royal Palace. Yet it is beyond the borders of this triangle, not far from the bustling city, where our guided tour through the land of asking must end. Our final destination is a tranquil space where art and nature co-exist in perfect harmony: Le Jardin Marjorelle.

As we wander along the leafy lanes, past the soothing streams and enchanting pools filled with water lilies and lotus flowers, we should take a moment to remind ourselves why it is we set out on our travels. To ask is natural. As natural as the rustling leaves and chirping birds taking refuge in this calming retreat. The purpose of asking is to create ideas as resonant as they are compelling, to nurture the imaginative and distinctive, to cut away the brambles that entrap ideas and liberate their creators.

Like the magical Gardens of Marjorelle, this book is a celebration of colour and creativity. It is a rejection of the black and white, yes-no world of market research. It is a passionate plea for you to experience your time in the land of asking with wide-eyed wonder, rather than through the narrow-minded lens of critical analysis and performance data. Our travels should be a journey of discovery and delight. Whether you prefer to amble along or sightsee with rigour and determination, my only wish is that you drink in the views, enjoy the contradictions and observe, embrace and appreciate the glory of intelligent response in all its complexity and colour.

END OF PART THREE

The sight of books removes sorrow from the heart

Moroccan proverb

Epilogue

The Art of Asking

I was feeling fragile when I got back from our weekend away, so I decided to go to the doctor.

The receptionist asked me what the matter was. I said, 'I think I've got Marrakesh Syndrome.'

'Sounds serious,' she replied. 'Take a seat in the waiting room. One of the doctors will be with you as soon as possible.' She handed me a small piece of paper, adding, 'Could you fill out this short survey and pop it in the box when you are done.'

I looked at the form and my heart sank.

THE FRIENDS AND FAMILY TEST

How likely are you to recommend our GP practice to family and friends?

Extremely Likely	Likely	Neither likely or unlikely	Unlikely	Extremely Unlikely	Don't know
☐	☐	☐	☐	☐	☐

Thinking about your response to this question, what is the main reason why you feel this way?

Clutching the expectant slip of paper, I wandered into the waiting room. It was packed. I squeezed into the last remaining seat between a woman with a bandage wrapped around her badly bitten tongue and a pale young man with a tear-stained face, who turned to me and asked plaintively, 'Why? Why didn't I dilute the squash?' Immediately opposite was a gentleman in his early fifties wearing a bright red baseball cap emblazoned with the slogan 'Telling is Selling'. I asked him where he got it from. He said a friend had picked it up at a conference.

'Did she have blue hair?' I enquired.

'How did you know?' he asked, amazed.

'Just a guess,' I said. 'Call it gut instinct.'

I filled out the form with a watered-down version of what I really thought. Then I popped it in the bin, not the box. If I have to hold back, what's the point?

My attention turned to the extraordinary array of advertising that adorned the walls of the busy surgery. The first thing that caught my eye was a black-and-white poster of a scrawny cat with a bolt through its head. It was heart-breaking. And yet, it was an image of cruelty so shocking I couldn't read on and instantly disconnected from the cause. Next to it was a clever, if long-winded poster from NHS Stop Smoking Services inviting smokers to read the message until they ran out of breath. 'Wishful thinking,' I mumbled to myself. There was a remedy for idea indigestion, called the ACID test, and a tasty new cookbook entitled 'Diet for the Healthy Heart'. I even recognised an old *Meet the Superhumans* poster from the London 2012 Paralympics. I loved that campaign. I honestly believe it changed the way people think about disability sport. Maybe forever.

And then, finally, my eyes alighted on a plain poster with a bright red title:

The Art of Asking

Intrigued, I read on.

Tired of being messed around by other people's opinions?
Sign up to our three-part course in Art Therapy.

Part One explains how to paint a picture of response.
Part Two covers composition and song.
Part Three concentrates on technique.

Alternatively, buy the book
'Asking for Trouble'
from your local bookshop.
It's packed with invaluable lessons
from a lifetime of listening.

I couldn't believe it. It was exactly what I was looking for. I ran out of the doctors' surgery, past Leonardo's Chicken Shack, past Cook, past the fez shop and into the bookstore in Muswell Hill.[22]

'Do you have a book called *Asking for Trouble*?' I panted.

'We've sold out,' the shop assistant answered. 'It's been surprisingly popular for a book about market research.'

I bought the paperback on Amazon and it arrived the next morning. I devoured it in a day. You should read it yourself, but in case you don't get the chance, I'll give you a quick summary of what I learnt.

Asking is an art. It is about painting and composition. Painting a picture of meaning and composing a song of truth. Being an art, it is not perfect. The very act of asking inevitably and unavoidably redirects the response and makes demands on those being asked. Practising and developing your skills of painting and composition cannot guarantee success, but the harder you work and the more proficient you become, the better the decisions you will make. It all comes down to you.

That is what makes asking so challenging, endlessly fascinating, enlightening and richly rewarding.

The world of asking will never be trouble-free, but as you jump on your magic carpet and fly off to a fantastical land of wonder and desire, at least you can be sure of one thing: you are in control of the direction and destiny of your idea, and your future is in nobody else's hands but your own. And that is a pretty good place to start.

THE END

IMAGE CREDITS

NOTES

1   A study by Shikhar Ghosh, senior lecturer at Harvard Business
    School, found that close to 75% of start-ups fail to return their
    investment. The late Clay Christensen, also of Harvard Business
    School, suggested the figure could be as high as 95%. Of the 660,000
    businesses registered in the UK every year, it is estimated that 60%
    will shut down within three years. Whether the exact figure is 60%,
    80% or 95%, one thing is for sure; most businesses don't make it.

2   Line used by permission of Ray Bradbury Literary Works, LLC

3   https://www.telegraph.co.uk/finance/newsbysector/
    retailandconsumer/11234229/How-McDonalds-was-turned-around-
    in- the-UK.html

4   Loftus, E. F., & Palmer, J. C. (1974). *Reconstruction of automobile
    destruction: An example of the interaction between language and
    memory. Journal of verbal learning and verbal behaviour.*
    https://edition.cnn.com/2013/05/18/health/lifeswork-loftus-memory-
    malleability/index.html

5   Reproduced by permission of Cancer Research UK

6   Abridged versions of the actual policy statements taken into research

7   *Creature Comforts* https://en.wikipedia.org/wiki/Creature_Comforts

8   The *Creature Discomforts* advertising received an overwhelmingly
    positive reception and generated a great deal of conversation.
    However, in the years since, some members of the disabled
    community have fed back to Leonard Cheshire that they were not
    comfortable with the way in which disabled people were depicted in
    the campaign.

9   *Superhumans* 2016
    https://www.youtube.com/ watch?v=IocLkk3aYlk

10 Used by permission of Richard Hamilton
    The Last Storytellers: Tales from the Heart of Morocco
    Published by I.B. Tauris 251

11 *In Arabian Nights* by Tahir Shah
    Published Feb. 11. 2008. by Bantam Books

12 Tom's idea: Used by permission of Tom Carver
    Nikki's idea: Used by permission of Nikki Wilkinson

Jack's idea: Tried to track down whose idea it was, without success. Jane's ideas. My idea really. Terrific idea.

13   *The psychological consequences of money*
     Authors: Kathleen D. Vohs, Nicole L. Mead, Miranda R. Goode.
     Source: Science, New series, Vol. 314, No. 5802, Nov. 17. 2006.
     pp 1154-1156 Published by American Association for the
     advancement of Science

14   *Impact of money on emotional expression.*
     Authors: Jiang, Y., Chen, Z., & Wyer, R. S., Jr. (2014).
     Source: Journal of Experimental Social Psychology, 55, 228–233.

     Both studies cited in an article by Joe Pinsker
     https://www.theatlantic.com/business/archive/2014/10/just-looking-
     at-money-makes-people-selfish-and-less-social/382088/

15   Used by permission of Rightmove PLC

16   From the *Muqaddimah of Ibn Khaldun* written in 1377.

     The 14th Century philosopher Ibn Khaldun is widely considered
     to be the founding father of Social Sciences.

17   Moroccan proverbs sourced from: http://www. special dictionary.
     com/proverbs/source/m/moroccan_proverb

18   Inspired by *Zoolander*. Very silly film. Recommended.

19   I have not personally conducted research on Toxocara. I came
     across this ad while searching for local government behaviour
     change campaigns to be used as stimulus for a project on behalf of
     Resource London.

20   The testing of these ads was undertaken by Nicki Karet of Sherbert
     Research. Finn and friends saw an earlier iteration of the Respect
     campaign.

21   *Predictably Irrational* by Dan Ariely is one of three books that have
     had a significant impact on my understanding of behaviour and
     response. Predictably, the other two are *Thinking Fast and Slow* by
     Daniel Kahneman and *Nudge* by Richard Thaler and Cass Sunstein.

22   There isn't really a Fez shop in Muswell Hill. Yet.

Acknowledgements

Firstly, thank you to those who have entrusted me with their asking. I've been lucky enough to work with many wonderful clients on the most interesting of projects. Special thanks to James Stevens for your encouragement and advice. Thanks to my colleagues, old and new, particularly Nicki Karet, Alex Maule, Richard Head, Nick Radley, Francis Sinclair, Debby Konigsberg and Imogen Baker.

Thanks to those who helped make this book possible. Justine Solomons of Byte the Book who pointed me in the right direction. My outstanding production team: editor Bryony Sutherland, cover designer Jack Smyth and interior designer Adam Hay. And of course, ever patient graphic designer and friend, Steve Stanton. Thanks to my readers, Imogen, Sarah, Brian, Isabel and James. This book is better for your input.

To my mum and dad, siblings, nieces, nephews, in-laws and friends, I love you all.

To my boys, what would I do without you? You are the wonders of my world and the soundtrack to my life. And never a moment's trouble! No one has ever been more blessed, nor could any father be more proud. And finally, thank you to my wife who has shared this journey with me. I could wish for no other travelling companion. You have given me everything that is good, and words cannot express how grateful I am. Thank you.

About the author

Jon has spent 25 years helping businesses, government and charities better understand their audiences, enabling them to make good decisions, produce great ideas, develop effective policies, and create compelling marketing communications. Jon is managing partner of consumer insight company Kindling. He sold his first research company, Rosenblatt, to the Cello Group in 2007. He lives in North London with his wife, four sons and a dog.